LONDON LANES

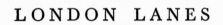

Love Lane, Aldermanbury.

LONDON LANES
BY ALAN STAPLETON
ILLUSTRATED WITH FORTY PENCIL
DRAWINGS BY THE AUTHOR

LONDON: JOHN LANE THE BODLEY HEAD LTD.
NEW YORK: DODD, MEAD AND COMPANY

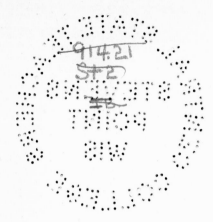
First published in 1930

Made and Printed in Great Britain.   Text by Butler & Tanner Ltd., Frome and London
Illustrations by George Gibbons & Co., Leicester

PREFACE

THIS BOOK NEEDS NO EXCUSE. IT IS AN ATTEMPT TO enumerate, name and describe, as far as possible, all the lanes—old and new—of London. I have discovered considerably over nine hundred names of these lanes, actually, at some time, or now, so called. Many are still in existence.

The earliest lanes, undoubtedly, were the paths between, and land approaches to, the inns, town-houses, palaces, and monasteries; also the lanes which led to the villages in the country beyond the walls of the city.

Some London streets were themselves but footways, or bridle-lanes, between the walls of the gardens belonging to the great houses of the nobles and palaces of the Kings; which houses, in order to preserve their privacy, were approached by their own barges to their own stairs on the river which they hugged—the river which had been the great means of transport for sixteen centuries.

Of these stairs a few still remain—with their approaches, termed 'lanes'. TRIG LANE comes into my mind at the moment; the narrow way from the old Trig stairs to Upper Thames Street. A sketch of this is in my *London Alleys, Byways, and Courts*.

The removal of the mansions of the nobles with their spacious grounds and courts, their conversion into smaller tenements, and the energetic building which went on in the sixteenth and seventeenth centuries were the causes of the formation of the innumerable small courts, yards, and alleys. These are now being rapidly crushed out by huge buildings or offices, blocks of offices, banks and warehouses.

Many of the old lanes, though retaining their original

names, have acquired, or have been promoted to, the dignity of being called 'roads' or 'streets'. It would be a pity should the description, memories and associations connected with them be as quickly forgotten as is bound to be the case with their old familiar appearance.

To trace all the lanes through the centuries, through all the changes caused by great fires, demolitions partial and entire, renomenclature and other happenings seemed to me to be of interest.

To endeavour to enumerate them all, to place them in their correct settings—topographic, historic and romantic —has been of still further interest.

Here are the results of my researches, together with forty drawings from my own pencil, made on the spot.

I can but hope that they may meet with as much kindly appreciation and friendly chaff as did my delvings into *London Alleys, Byways, and Courts*. For more than that I could not wish. The long-threatened second volume of that work will appear in due course.

Ill luck has been present with me again, even in this book of Lanes.

Many of my notes and drawings for it were destroyed by fire; as well as a quantity of the first Edition of my *London Alleys, Byways, and Courts*. To breast the blow of circumstance and grapple with my evil star was necessary. I crave indulgence for any sins of omission and of commission in this the net result of my attempt.

In the course of this attempt I have, as I said in the preface to my *London Alleys, Byways, and Courts*, levied toll upon nearly everyone who has written a book upon London.

I hope to be forgiven?

Anyway, I tender to each one my hearty thanks.

ALAN STAPLETON.

LIST OF ILLUSTRATIONS

LONDON LANES

LONDON LANES

CHAPTER I

LONDON LANES—ONCE OLD, FAMILIAR LITTLE PLACES.
Not like some of our new great streets—the
essence of grandiloquence, altiloquence, magnificence, and every other sense except that intimate sense of the warmth of human associations
and memories which is now being continually sent to
limbo.

The old lanes are rapidly being replaced by thorough-
fares lined with cold, stone giants which hug the sky and
live in the clouds, as if they have risen superior to human
interest.

In the time of Henry VIII and Elizabeth the houses of
London certainly climbed skywards along the narrow
lanes. These houses were half-timbered buildings of sometimes eight storeys. But each storey bulged out over the
next lower, so that the people on the topmost storey could
almost shake hands with their neighbours across the way.

Up to the end of the eighteenth century the citizens of
London lived in the heart of their city—over their business
premises, chiefly. This is proved by the evidence of old
records, documents and maps.

The city—then their stronghold—has now degenerated
into a mere postal district. It no longer possesses any

bars, gates, walls or visible bounds. And but few people, other than office-keepers and caretakers, reside in it.

Many of the old lanes which ran along the backs of houses and between gardens still remain. Their names tell the history of their origin. South of St. Paul's and Cheapside, where the lanes slope down to the river, are many such.

From 77 Queen Victoria Street to Upper Thames Street runs FYEFOOT LANE, a very slight variation in the spelling from the lane which Stow explained was called FINIMORE LANE or FIVEFOOT LANE because it is but five feet in breadth at the west end. Roberts in his *New Review of London*, 1728, gives it as FYFOOD LANE. In 1316 Philip le Bret demised to his son a tenement with a shop in the parish of St. Nicholas Olof in a street called FYNAMOURES-LANE. It is called FOOT LANE in a 1773 map.

FIVE FOOT LANE was the old name for Russell Street, Bermondsey, according to a letter from 'Ambulator' to the *Gentleman's Magazine*, 1798, Part II, pp. 647–9. There is still an Upper Russell Street at 106 Bermondsey Street; but Russell Street (almost a continuation) has evidently been changed to Tanner Street; for, looking at the configuration of Five Foot Lane in the 1772 plan of London, Westminster, and Southwark engraved for Noorthouck's *History*, it is identical with Tanner Street. Both start from Bermondsey Street and both end at St. Saviour's Dock.

A FIFTEENFEET LANE is given in Large's *Way about London* as being the first turning on the right in King's Cross Road from Pentonville Road. This would be the now Pakenham Street. St. Chad's Well—long one of the favourite spas—was in this lane.

The Church of St. Mary, Mounthaunt, or Mounthaw, burnt in the Great Fire of 1666 and not rebuilt, stood on the east side of Old Fish Street Hill. On the west side of the Hill was an ancient large-roomed house, built of stone and timber, once belonging to the Mounthaunts of Norfolk. They sold it in 1234 to Radulphus de Maydenstone, Bishop of Hereford. He gave it to the Bishops of Hereford, his successors. A lane by this church—at first a very small chapel for the Mounthaunts' house—was named after it. Stow tells us that on the east side of it is another lane, turning east through St. Nicholas Olave's Churchyard to Bread Street Hill, Finimore or Fivefoot Lane, and that 'In the middle of this lane runneth one lane broader, South to Thames Street. I think the same to be called. DESBOURNE LANE, for I read of such a lane to have been in the parish of St. Mary Summerset in the 22nd year of Edward III.'

The main portion of Old Fish Street Hill was destroyed for the formation of Queen Victoria Street, and the remaining portion since 1909 has been called Lambeth Hill.

Harben explains that Desbourne Lane was mentioned in the seventeenth year of Edward III, when a view was held of precincts of the Thames and inquiry made as to certain lanes which were intended for public use, but had to be shut up at various times by owners of property in them. Sir Edward de Montacute's house was on the east side, Walter Gladewyn's on the west.

ACRE LANE runs from Brixton Hill to Clapham Park Road. FORTY ACRE LANE runs into Denmark Street, Barking Road, Plaistow. Off Barking Road, nearly oppo-

site Denmark Street, is a lane curiously named CHARGE-
ABLE LANE.

A TREE IN POUND LANE runs off PRINCE REGENT'S LANE,
which runs into Dock Road, Victoria Dock.

WHITE POST LANE runs from Barking Road to Romford
Road at East Ham.

A SEVENFOOT LANE was on the west side of IRONMONGER
LANE. It was called, in 1354, SENEHODES LANE, in 1376
SEPHOD LANE, and SEVENFOTELANE in 1457. A Henry
Sevehod living in Ironmonger Lane in 1283 may have
given the name to the smaller lane, perhaps his property.
The only turning on the west side, now, appears to be
Prudent Passage.

At the west end of St. Michael's, Queenhithe, was a lane
called PYEL LANE, according to Stow.

In the parish of this same St. Michael's was DIBLESLANE,
in which in 1301 a certain Richard Hardel owned rents.
In 1310 Stephen, son of Henry de Coventre, in his will
excepted the reversion of a tenement and wharf in this
lane, which he left to his child en ventre sa mère.

Nearly opposite Fyefoot Lane was a lane with the
salubrious name of DUNGHILL LANE. Dunghill Lane is
marked in Noorthouck's map, 1772, as immediately north
of Old Baynard's Castle and HAMOND'S LANE. This is
now called High Timber Street. A lane near King's Cross
(to be described later) was called MAIDEN LANE. This was
an improvement upon its previous name of MIDDEN LANE,
that having been the change from Dunghill Lane.

At the corner of High Timber Street, east of Broken
Wharf, is GARDNER'S LANE. Lyon's Wharf is at the end
of the lane. On the right side entering, as late as 1856,

there used to be a bas-relief of a gardener with a spade (full length) with date 1760. This is now in the Guildhall Museum—rather crude work. Mr. J. T. Smith says tradition has it that the site was once gardens.

GARDENER's LANE was in Westminster, between old King and Duke Streets; marked in Noorthouck's map of 1772 as being then the fifth turning on the right from the Horse Guards. In the same map is shown a GARDINER LANE, running from Petty France to Little Chapel Street, Westminster. Petty France is now named York Street.

In one of these two lanes Wenceslaus Hollar, the engraver, died. Aubrey found the register of his death at St. Margaret's Church, but Jesse in his *Memorials of London* says his remains lie in the burying-ground attached to the 'New Chapel' in 'Petty France'.

Rocque's 1747 map gives a GARDINER's LANE near Willow Street, Southwark.

TRIG LANE is one of the old, narrow lanes leading to the river-stairs of the same name. This was called after Sir John Trigge, owner of the stairs in the reign of Edward III, opposite Lambeth Hill, and at 34 Upper Thames Street.

In the Puppet Show of Hero and Leander in Ben Jonson's *Bartholomew Fair:*

> Leander does ask, Sir, what fairest of fairs
> Was the fare he landed but now at Trig Stairs.

A few yards eastwards is STEW LANE. This has been known by two other names—HAMOND's LANE and PARKER-ISLANE, and is the narrow passage which led to Stew Quay, from which embarked the ladies who, in the time of Edward III, were ordered to 'wear striped hoods of party colours and their garments the wrong side outwards', on their passage across the Thames to the 'Bordello' or 'Stews', which allowed houses had signs painted on their fronts towards the river, such as a 'Boar's Head', the 'Cross Keys', the 'Gun', the 'Bell', the 'Swan', the 'Cranes', the 'Castle', the 'Cardinal's Hat', etc.

The two latter were mentioned in the expenses of Sir John Howard, the first Duke of Norfolk of that name.

Chronicler Stow quaintly gives the derivation of Stew Lane—'of a stew or hothouse there kept'. These stews were as old as the reign of Henry II, and in Richard II's reign belonged to Sir William Walworth. Many of these houses were destroyed by Wat Tyler, who received a tit-for-tat (or *tête*) at Smithfield on that day in June when the worthy Mayor, being himself struck with amazement at Wat Tyler's insolence to the King, struck him with a mace.

It should be remembered that Wat Tyler's insurrection was caused by one of the collectors of the Poll Tax, levied in 1379, being indecently rude to Wat Tyler's daughter, for the purpose, as the collector said, of proving she was of age (15) to pay the tax. He was struck dead by Tyler.

DARKHOUSE LANE is next east to Stew Lane. In Noorthouck's map it is marked DARK LANE. In 1355, Wm. de Thame, blader, left a granary in LE DERKELANE in the parish of St. Michael, Queenhithe, to his daughters, Agnes and Alice.

Nearly opposite Darkhouse Lane is HUGGIN LANE. This was found by Riley to have existed under the name of HOGGENLANE as far back as 1281. But in 1275 a Richard Bonaventure demised a house in Hoggenlane, held on mortgage to be sold for payment of debts. In its south-east corner stood the Church of St. Michael, Queenhithe.

St. Michael Hoggen Lane is mentioned in the *Calendar of Wills*, I, 514. A tenement there, named le Blakegate, which belonged in 1348 to Henry de Iddesworth, Arch-deacon of Middlesex, and Canon of St. Paul's, was be-queathed by him for maintenance of a chantry in the Cathedral.

Stow says Huggin Lane was called Spuren or Spooner's Lane, but gives no reason. In a will in 1353 it is called 'Sporoneslane in the Ward of Queenhithe'.

Another Huggin Lane runs from Wood Street, Cheap-side, to Gutter Lane;—so called of one Hugan that of old time dwelt there. 'He was called "Hugan in the lane", as I have read, in The 34th of Edward I', says Stow.

Next east to Huggin Lane, Upper Thames Street, is Little Trinity Lane, in which is the Painter Stainer's Hall. This existed as a fraternity long before 1580, but there was no charter of incorporation before then. Orders were made to compel foreign painters then resident in London, Steenwych, Gentileschi, etc., to pay fines for following their art without being free of the Painter Stainer's Co. The lane was widened in George II's time by the houses at the north-east corner, near the old Dog Tavern, being pulled down and the ground laid into the street.

In Edward III's time, John, Earl of Cornwall, owned a great messuage on the east side of the lower end of Little Trinity Lane.

Great Trinity Lane runs along the top of the latter. Both these lanes were so called from the Church of the

Holy Trinity, destroyed in the Great Fire and not rebuilt, but united to St. Michael's, Queenhithe. Off Queenhithe on the left was a lane called PUMP LANE. This ran into TOWNS-END LANE, leading from 66 Upper Thames Street to Bull's Wharf. It is now called BULL's WHARF LANE. A TOWNSEND LANE is mentioned by Roberts in his *New View of London*, 1708, in connection with a CORPORATION LANE, between the former lane and St. John Street, near Hockley-in-the-Hole. Corporation Lane tallies with the present Row of that name.

Then was ANCHOR LANE, now Anchor Alley, leading to the wharf of the same name—the place where on June 30th, 1557, Henry Machyn, the diarist, and some friends, 'did eat half a bushell of owsturs in Anchor Lane at Master Smith and Master Gytton's cellar, upon hogshead and candlelight, and onions and red ale, and claret ale, and muscadell and malmsey ale, free cope, at 8 in the morning'. Good, though quaint customs of nearly four hundred years ago!

The old name for Anchor Lane was PALMER'S LANE. The Plumbers had their hall there, but were tenants to the Vintners.

In *Domestic Papers* (*Calendar of State Papers*), 1661–2, p. 87, reference is made to a conventicle in this Lane 'where two pulpits are set up for prophesying'.

In the Post Office List for 1857, an Anchor Lane is given as being in Mile End Road. I cannot trace it.

THREE CRANES LANE, just east of Vintners Hall, keeps in memory and is on the site of the tavern, famous as early as the reign of James I, frequented by the wits in Ben Jonson's time. In *Bartholomew Fair* he says: 'A pox o' these pretenders to wit, your Three Cranes, Mitre and Mermaid men! Not a corn of true salt, not a grain of right mustard among them all!'

People usually walked from this tavern to Billingsgate, leaving their boats outside to shoot the bridge; after rejoining their boats they would take to water again.

Referring to this lane—'Taken up by Costermongers', says Strype in his 1720 edition. 'Taken up by Fruiterers', says he in his 1755 edition. So he knew the Costard apples, 'round and bulky like the head' from which costermongers took their name.

It was really named from three strong cranes of timber placed on Vintry Wharf, to unload wines. The sign of three birds was in the punning jocularity of the times. In the ninth of Richard II this lane was called the PAINTED TAVERN LANE of the tavern being painted.

BRICKHILL LANE, the next eastwards, is so called, says Lockie, because there was once a mound of clay there, from which bricks were made.

Stow tells us—'Now, on the Thames Side, west from GRANTHAM's LANE, have ye HERBER's LANE or BRIKEL's LANE, so called of John Brikels, sometime owner thereof'. This John Brikel left an annual sum of £9 for prayers for his soul.

EMPEROR's HEAD LANE of such a sign, or SIMPSON's LANE, of one Simpson, next to Brikel's Lane, was the present BELL WHARF LANE, described as south out of Upper Thames Street to Greenwich Street and Bell Wharf, formerly Emperor's Head Lane. Fisherman's Hall, mentioned in a deed of 1741 relating to houses in Brickel's Charity, is identified with the 'Emperor's Head' here.

After the Great Fire the buildings on the west side were set back a foot and a half to widen the alley. It was not found possible to set back those on the east side. The old-termed TENNIS COURT LANE next it must be the present BREWER'S LANE, out of which runs FRYERS LANE, now 'Fryer's Alley'. This latter was called GREENEWICH LANE in olden times. In it were the Joiner's Hall and other fair houses. The Walbrook emptied itself into the Thames down this lane. Stow says it was called FRIER LANE, because of such a sign there set up.

LITTLE ELBOW LANE ran into ELBOW LANE on the north side of Upper Thames Street nearly opposite Brewer's Lane. The former is now called Little College Street and the latter College Street. Dodsley mentions a GREAT and Little Elbow Lane and a Naked Boy Court running out of one of them.

There is another Elbow Lane to the left out of NEW GRAVEL LANE in Shadwell High Street. This Elbow Lane has an elbow turning to the left again, then up a few steps back into the High Street at No. 30.

COUSIN LANE, next to Dowgate, dates from the days of Edward I, probably, since it was named after 'William Cosin, one of the sheriffs in the year 1306 who dwelt there, as divers his predecessors, father, grandfather, etc., had done before him'. His house stood at the bottom of the lane, and had an old and artificial conveyance of Thames water into it. It was afterwards, in Stow's days, a dyehouse called Lambard's messuage. At that time there had lately been erected—adjoining the house—an engine to convey the water into Downegate conduit.

In her will in 1305–6 Johanna Cosyn left her houses in

New Grand Lane
Wapping

the lane called LA COSYNESLANE to be sold; and wished certain relations to benefit thereby. Between this and ALL HALLOWS LANE was a narrow way into a large old house in Upper Thames Street next to the Guildhall, belonging to the merchants of Haunce who hired this house, once belonging to a famous lapidary named Richard Lions. He was one of the sheriffs of London in Edward III's time and was dragged out of this house by the rebels of Kent in the early days of Richard II and beheaded in West Cheap. This narrow way was called WINDGOOSE, WANDGOOSE, or WILDGOOSE LANE.

Old CHURCH LANE is now ALLHALLOWS LANE, by the side of where stood the Church called Allhallows-the-More in Thames Street (demolished in 1895), and comes before HAY WHARF LANE, in which was a great brewery built by one Pot; Henry Campion, esquire, a beer-brewer, used it; then his son, Abraham. It is now the City of London Brewery.

The next lane is OLD SWAN LANE, the furthest point to which fishermen on the north bank of the Thames in the old days of the fourteenth century were allowed to come by a provision in the regulations of the Committee of Free Fishermen.

At Swan Stairs people were accustomed to land to walk to the other side of London Bridge, where there was such a swift and narrow current between the starlings that it was rather like shooting the rapids to venture. The boat was usually taken again at Billingsgate, as it was by Johnson and Boswell on their famous trip to Greenwich. Lampreys used to be caught in great quantities below bridge.

Next to Old Swan Lane was EBGATE LANE. The Ebgate was also called The Oystergate. Probably a tidal gate. For old Stow says: 'The next is Ebgate, a water gate so called of old time, as appeareth by divers records of tenements near unto the same adjoining. It standeth next unto the Church of St. Laurence Pountney. . . . In place of the gate is now a narrow passage leading to the Thames, and is called Ebgate Lane, but more commonly the Old Swan.' This is now SWAN LANE and was probably renamed so because the keeper of the Bridge-master's swans had his office near here.

To keep swans on the Thames was esteemed a privilege, at present exercised only by the Crown and the companies of the Dyers and the Vintners. Why the Corporation ceased to exercise their privilege does not appear. The mark in use for the Bridge Swans was lost. Accounts for June, 1434, show expenses for marking the King's swans; for the hire of two men navigating two boats at Stratford for the swans; for a breakfast which formed the usual accompaniment to the 'swan upping'; for a swan mark entered in the King's book, and for services of the Swan-master's men in following many swans for the bridge.

A manuscript of the fourth of Richard II shows that all swans coming through London Bridge became the property of Constables of the Tower; the owner of every swan nesting beneath the Bridge paid him a cygnet out of every nest.

A Swan Lane in Bermondsey starts at 168 Rotherhithe Street. Yet another one was in Old Brompton Road.

A short distance along Lower Thames Street on the north side is PUDDING LANE, which has had many names.

Swan Lane

In the will of Thomas Beaumond, Salter, dated 1452, he mentions 'FYNKESLANE in the Parish of St. George near Estchepe and St. Andrew Hubbard', and refers to it as 'near the lane lately called Fynkeslane and now called PODYNGLANE'. This must be entirely distinct from the Finch, Fynkis or Fynkes Lane off Cornhill. Stow gives ROTHER LANE or RED ROSE LANE of such a sign there, but says it is now commonly called Pudding Lane because 'the butchers of Eastcheap have their scalding houses for hogs there, and their puddings and other filth of beast are voided down that way to the dung boats on the Thames'. In his time it was chiefly inhabited by basket makers, turners and butchers.

The great conflagration of 1666 started here at the house of Farryner, the King's baker, between 1 and 2 a.m. on Sunday, September the 2nd. The houses were of wood, overhanging the roadway. The season was unusually dry, and a strong east wind was blowing. It was thought little of at first. Pepys put his head out of his window in Seething Lane and went back to bed. Sir Thomas Bludworth, then Lord Mayor, also thought little of it until too late. The fire raged for four days. Houses were pulled down and blown up, but the flames still spreading west were finally stopped at the Temple Church and at Pie Corner in West Smithfield, where a copy of a statuette representing a naked boy still adorns the corner of COCK LANE. On the breast and arms of the original figure were the curious words: 'This boy is in Memory put up for the Late Fire of London, occasioned by the Sin of Gluttony. 1666.'

These words once were a source of inspiration to a Nonconformist preacher on the anniversary of the Fire. He declared that the sin of blasphemy could not have caused the fire, for in that case it would have commenced at Billingsgate; that since it did not begin in Drury Lane, the cause was not the sin of wantonness nor lewdness; nor by the sin of lying, for then the flames had started from Westminster Hall. 'No, my brethren; it was caused by the sin of gluttony, for it began at Pudding Lane and ended at Pie Corner!'

Ben Jonson in his *Masque of Christmas*, 1616, makes Venus say: 'Right, forsooth, I am Cupid's mother. . . . I dwell in Pudding Lane.'

In the will of Richard le Rus, in 1279, it is called REDERISGATE LANE. The LANE OF ST. MARGARET NEAR REDERESGATE is mentioned in the will of John Jukel, goldsmith, in 1284, whereby he leaves to Henry his son, rents there. REDDERISGATELANE is mentioned as being in the parish of St. Margaret de Bruggestrate (Bridge Street) in the will of Robert le Rus, in 1279. In that of Robert de Mockyng, fishmonger, 1322, it is termed RETHERESGATES-LANE, and in Richard Swote's will it is referred to as ROTHERESGATESLANE, a change of but one letter. Shortened to RETHERESLANE in the will of 1349 of Johann Youn, who leaves to her Canons and Convent of the Church of Holy Trinity, London, for providing medicines, her tenements here. It is mentioned yet earlier as REDERES-LANE in the will, dated 1301, of Margery Bachelor. There is a Pudding Lane past Bow Bridge to Pudding Mill Rise.

BOTOLPH'S LANE is the next lane east of Pudding Lane. In the calendar of letters and papers during the Commonwealth it was called BOTTLE LANE, named after St. Botolph's Church, Billingsgate. The Wharf at the bottom

Love Lane, Monument.

is the site of the foot of old London Bridge. The last of
the Fitz-Alans, Earls of Arundel, who died in 1579, had
a house in this lane.

The old Church of St. George in the lane was destroyed
in the Great Fire. The name is preserved in GEORGE
LANE, which runs from Pudding Lane to Botolph Lane.
In 1669 the father of Bishop Sherlock had the rectory of
the new church erected by Sir Christopher Wren, finished
in 1674.

LOVE LANE (one of nine of that name in London) runs
from Monument Street up to Eastcheap, at which end of
the lane stood the King's Weigh House built on the
ground where stood the Church of St. Andrew Hubbard
before the fire; the weigh house was in Cornhill previously. Here merchandise from beyond the seas was
weighed by the King's beam, to which belonged a Master
and four master-porters with labouring porters under
them.

The Church in Love Lane serves the united parishes of
St. Mary at Hill, St. Andrew Hubbard, and St. George
Botolph Lane with St. Botolph of Billingsgate.

Sir Christopher Wren lived in the large house (now
divided into two) with the steps. A fee of threepence used
to be charged for viewing the fine oak staircase, now
vanished.

SMITHER'S LANE was the name given to that part of the
present Eastcheap between Botolph and ROOD LANES,
before the Fire. SMETHELANE is mentioned in a will of
1282, by Richard le Mouner, who left a house there to
his brother William. In the will of Juliana Box, 1325,
Smethelane is described as being in the parish of All

Hallows de Berkyngecherche. From Botolph Lane across Love Lane we come to IDOL (sometimes written IDLE) LANE, running from Tower Street to St. Dunstan's Hill. In Stow's time this lane was called CHURCH LANE, while the short lane between it and St. Mary-at-Hill was called FOWLE LANE, now CROSS LANE. 'Foul' might well have been the correct spelling! Fowle Lane was the name of CHICKINE LANE in 1546, the previous names of which were CHICKE, STINKING and STINKENDELANE in 1285, BUTCHER HALL LANE in Stow's time, and, as elsewhere mentioned, since 1843 renamed King Edward Street after Edward VI in commemoration of his interest in Christ's Hospital.

Before Monument Street was formed this Love Lane off it extended to Lower Thames Street. It has had other names. Of old it was called ROAPE LANE, since called LUCAS LANE, of one Lucas, owner of some part thereof, and now, as Stow puts it, corruptly called Love Lane. Although that must have been some time ago. For in the *Calendar of Wills, Court of Husting*, it is mentioned in 1394 as Love Lane, formerly called ROPPELANE near Billingsgate.

Harben tells us that in connection with the name Love Lane about the year 1377 in an ordinance for safeguarding the City, the Alderman of Billynges-gate Ward was to guard the wharf of Reynold Love up to Billinges-gate. It does not seem impossible, therefore, that the change of name from Roper to Love may have been made about this time, and that the lane may have been renamed after this family, if, as it seems, they were possessed of considerable property in the neighbourhood. A suggestion made in *Notes and Queries* is that the lane was named

Idol Lane

corruptly after John Lovken (or Lovekyn), the Stock Fishmonger, who was four times Mayor of London from 1348
to 1358. This lane ran up by the east end of the old
parish church of St. Andrew Hubbard, or St. Andrew in
East Cheap. ST. ANDREW HUBBARD'S LANE is mentioned
several times in thirteenth- and fourteenth-century documents.

Another Love Lane runs from Wood Street, Cheapside,
to Aldermanbury. By St. Alban's Church there is LITTLE
LOVE LANE. This Love Lane is first mentioned by Stow
in his 1598 edition, p. 231. That part north and east of
the church now called Little Love Lane was called Love
Lane in both Strype's editions of 1720 and 1775, while in
New Remarks of London collected by the Parish Clerks, 1732,
part of it is called GREAT LOVE LANE.

Stow says, 'So called of wantons'. 'The amorous and
wanton Persons formerly here remarkable' is the comment
in another *New View of London*. As has been remarked
before, names of lanes tell the history of their origin.
Huggin Lane, in spite of the etymological explanation of
its name by Stow (mentioned previously), might have
another reason for being so called. It is very near this
Love Lane.

A third Love Lane was in Broad Sanctuary, Westminster, between the west end of the Abbey and Prince's
Street.

Another was in Rotherhithe Street opposite Rotherhithe
Stairs. A fifth remains in Sumner Street, Southwark, and
runs to Bankside. Another Love Lane runs from 117
Shadwell High Street to Brook Street. Brook Street runs
from Devonport Street to Whitehorse Street. In Brook

c

Street is SCHOOLHOUSE LANE. In Devonport Street is
STEEL'S LANE, to Harding Street. The next turning but
one to this Love Lane is KING DAVID'S LANE, which runs
through to Cable Street by the side of the Sun Tavern
Fields. There was a SUN TAVERN FIELDS LANE: I have not
discovered it. In an 1840 map a lane is shown, but unnamed, running through and across these fields. Yet
another was to be found in old Ratcliffe Highway (now
called St. George Street).

Love Lane was the old name for Paris and Little Paris
Streets, which skirt Lambeth Palace Garden from the
Embankment (Bishop's Walk) to opposite Upper Marsh.
From Stockwell Road to Sidney Street runs yet another
Love Lane.

In Rocque's map of 1763 a Love Lane is marked, a little
south of the Jew's Harp, which stood at about opposite
the top of Portland Place in Marylebone Park. This lane
led to it from the east and MARYLEBONE LANE north of the
turnpike from the south.

In Mogg's *London in Miniature* plan, published in 1840,
LOVING EDWARD LANE is marked as running between
TRUNDLEY'S LANE and the commencement of High Street,
Deptford. The situation has evidently improved there,
for the 'Loving' has been dropped and Lane has been
promoted to Street—Edward Street being now its name;
while Trundley's Lane is now Woodpecker Road at that
end—though the other end is still Trundley's Road, where
it joins the now Evelyn Street from New Road—of old
Deptford Lower Road. CONEY HILL LANE has been
wiped out. WINDMILL LANE is still marked on the P.O.
map. PLOUGH LANE has risen to Road and MANOR LANE

Long Lane, Borough

and CORBETTS LANE have become respectively Abbey-
field Road and New Road. BLUE ANCHOR LANE is still
shown, but Blue Anchor Road has become Southwark
Park Road. Blue Anchor Lane runs from 251 Southwark
Park Road to 117 St. James' Road, Bermondsey. At the
'Blue Anchor', at the corner, was the sign of Henry
Sherringham (d. 1703), publisher in Charles II's time.

Another Blue Anchor Lane runs from 119 High Street,
Peckham, to Goldsmith Road.

There are now two LONG LANES in London. Dodsley
gives one other in Shoreditch which I have not been able
to trace. There is a Long Street (which is exceedingly
short) from Union Street to Cremer Street near the end
of COCK LANE, Shoreditch. Of the two remaining Long
Lanes, that in the Borough is the longest; measuring
(according to Cary's *New Guide*, showing 'actual and minute
measurements of every street which is a carriage way
throughout the metropolis', published in 1801) four furlongs eight poles. 'It is a long lane that knows no turnings',
Browning wrote. This has twenty-one such. Between two
of them is a public-house with an uncommon name—the
'Valentine and Orson' was mentioned in the *Daily Courant*,
February 19th, 1711, as a coffee-house. That and another
one—facetiously said to be the only one mentioned in the
Bible, 'Simon the Tanner'—are still there. It will be recalled that Simon, whose surname was Peter, lodged in
the house of his namesake at Joppa, by the seaside.

Off this Long Lane is Tabard Street (Kent Street pre-
viously). Off Kent Street was a TRANCE'S LANE. TENTER
GROUND LANE ran off Blue Anchor Road, which is now
Southwark Park Road, and that old lane is now Reverdy

Street at 92 Southwark Park Road. Kent Street was the way taken by Chaucer's pilgrims. As early as the fourteenth century the Loke (afterwards Lock) Hospital for lepers stood there. An open stream called the Lock divided the parishes of St. George and St. Mary, Newington. LOCK FIELDS LANE ran west of Lock Fields into the New Road, now New Kent Road. The lane is marked in Rocque's 1763 map.

Kent Street had an evil reputation—'the worst-kept part of London—in a police-sense, of course—excepting the Haymarket' is the description in *The Uncommercial Traveller*.

The longest lane in London is BRICK LANE, Spitalfields. Hatton in 1708 called it the longest lane in London, being then nearly three-quarters of a mile long. But PARK LANE, by Hyde Park, was then six furlongs thirteen poles in length; so it had the advantage of Brick Lane, the length of which was five furlongs four poles. Brick Lane, by taking in its length its old continuations Tyssen Street and Turk's Street, now beats it by thirteen poles, Tyssen Street measuring one furlong fourteen poles, and Turk's Street eight poles; thus bringing the length of the present Brick Lane to six furlongs twenty-six poles. In Brick Lane is the brewery of Messrs. Truman Hanbury and Buxton. Hanbury Street next to it was old BROWN'S LANE. Off Brick Lane is Flower and Dean Street, at the west end of which, running from Fashion Street to Wentworth Street, was a ROSE LANE, marked in the 1840 map. It is now wiped out by Commercial Street.

WHITE HORSE LANE was undoubtedly the longest lane when it existed. It seems to have been wiped out to form Commercial Road. It ran from Church Lane, Whitechapel, past Stepney Causeway and Ratcliff Square to Whitehorse

Brick Lane, looking north.

Street, and Cary gives its length, in 1801, as one mile one furlong twelve poles. In a map dated 1829 that part of the present Commercial Road from Church Lane to Cannon Street Row is named White Horse Street.

A present-day White Horse Lane runs from Stepney Green to 264 Mile End Road. In the 1829 map this lane finishes at Trafalgar Square, and the northern end to Mile End Road is called George Street.

In old White Horse Lane, Westminster, Bishop Kennet says, lived one Wraithwood, who was very much suspected of being the executioner of Charles I.

Another White Horse Lane is off Barking Road at the junction with BLIND LANE, into which runs TUNMARSH LANE.

HORNSEY WOOD LANE was seven furlongs fifteen poles; DU VAL'S OR DEVIL'S LANE, Holloway, five furlongs fifteen poles; Church Lane, Kensington, five furlongs two poles.

Long Lane is also longer than it was as it has swallowed up White Street and Church Street and now extends to the Borough High Street instead of commencing at Crosby Row as in a map of 1829. Then it measured four furlongs eight poles. Since Church Street has sixteen poles to add, and White Street about the same, the lane now measures five furlongs.

In addition to the above-mentioned Brick Lane was one in Park Lane, Piccadilly. This has now been promoted to the dignity of 'Street'.

Brick Lane was the old name of Central Street, St. Luke's, from the north side of Old Street, continuation of GOLDEN LANE to City Road. It was so called only so far as the present Lever Street; from whence to City Road it was called York Street. Lever Street ate up old Wellington Street, St. John's Row and Ratcliff Row, from Goswell Street to Bath Street.

One of the Long Parliament's fortifications—a redoubt with two flanks—was at this Brick Lane.

Yet another Brick Lane. This is the name in an 1840 map of FROG LANE, which runs from City Road to New North Road. A LITTLE BRICK LANE is mentioned at Nicholl Street, Bethnal Green Road.

The other remaining Long Lane runs from West Smithfield to Aldersgate Street. Stow, in 1603, said: 'This lane is now lately built on both sides with tenements for brokers, tipplers, and such like.' But earlier than this, in Nash's *Pierce Pennilesse* (1592), we have—'The times are dangerous, and this is an yron age; or rather no yron age, for sworde and bucklers goe to pawne apace in Long Lane.' Stow remarked the lane was truly called 'Long'; but in length it compares badly, being but one furlong thirteen poles (as Cary has it), with the Borough one of the same name, previously described. Tom Brown in his *Amusement of London* declared that though he was always more scared at the sight of a serjeant or bayliff than at the Devil and all his works, yet he was 'mortally frightened' in his passage through Barbican and Long Lane by the impudent rag-sellers in those scandalous climates, who did lay hold of his arm to ask him what he lack'd. That was about 1700.

In 1634 a broker in the lane, named Cromes, was committed to the Marshalsea for sending a church robe, with the name of Jesus upon it, to the players in Salisbury Court, to present a Flamen—a priest of the heathens.

Dekker makes Birdlime say (in *Westward Ho*): 'The troth

Brick Lane, Bethnal Green,
looking south.

is, my Lord, I got her to my house . . . hired three liveries in Long Lane to man her.'

Morley tells us that on Bart's Fair day Long Lane looks 'very faire, and puts out her best cloaths with the wrong side outward, so turned for their better turning off'.

This lane once had as a resident Hogarth's father, who came from Northumberland. The artist was born (according to the Church records) 'next door to Mr. Downing's the printers in Bartholomew Close hard by'.

One of the oldest bits in the lane is the corner of Sun Court, see sketch.

In 1197 lands were described as lying by Smithfield Bar 'super rivulum Fackeswell, and other lands as between that brook and CHICKENNE LANE'. CHARTERHOUSE LANE was just outside the city to the east of the Bar, and Chickenne Lane just inside to the west. This latter was afterwards called West Street, in which was an infamous house called the 'Red Lion', figuring in Plate IX of Hogarth's *Industry and Idleness*, under the name of the Blood-Bowl house*— demolished in July, 1844. It overlooked the open descent of the Fleet from Clerkenwell to Farringdon Street, and was full of passages, trap-doors, sliding panels and cellars for convenience of thieves. A plank across the river often helped them to escape. Ned Ward in *London Spy* mentions: 'walk'd on till we came to the end of a little stinking lane, which my friend told me was Chick-Lane; where measly pork and neck-of-beef stood out in wooden platters, adorned with carrots, and garnished with the leaves of marigolds'. This was another lane which was first actually named STINKING LANE ('so called as leading to the slaughter-houses of St. Nicholas Shambles', says Stow)

* This was also said to be in Hanging Sword Alley, which see. Page 145.

before being called CHICK LANE. It was next known as
Blowbladder-Street; then BUTCHER-HALL LANE, because
the hall belonging to the Company of Butchers was there;
and finally, as now, King Edward Street. This would be
the 'Chykenall, Parish of St. Sepulchre' mentioned in
Johanna le Waley's will in 1282. A BUTCHER'S LANE off
Brent Street, Hendon, is marked in an 1895 map.

At the 'Three Jolly Pigeons' in Butcher-Hall Lane was
held the Cauliflower Club, members of which were mostly
booksellers from Paternoster Row. A large cauliflower
painted on the ceiling of the club-room represented the
head on the gallon of porter which was paid for by every
member who sat under it at his initiation. The President's
chair was sold at Christie's—one of Chippendale's master-
pieces—in 1874. It was adorned by an exquisitely carved
cauliflower at back and sides; the arms with leaves. Both
legs and arms were fluted. Made of solid dark Spanish
mahogany. By Act of Parliament in 1760, a passage 25 feet
wide was to be made from this lane into Little Britain.

In the Sessions of Peace Register under date 25 July,
ninth of James I, is an order

that there shalbe made a cage and a paire of Stockes for
St. John's Streete, Cowcrosse and Charterhouse Lane, the
Stockes to be perfectly made and sitt in their ancient place,
and the Cage in some other convenient place, and that the
Inhabitants of the severall places aforesaid to taxe the
residew towards theffecting thereof.

This Lane is now a Street.

CHIGENELANE, in the parish of All Hallows de Berkinge-
cherche, is mentioned in a will in 1301, of Martin Box,
alderman. This is evidently the lane Stow gives as being

'on the east of Barking Church, at the end whereof you have Tower Street stretching from the Tower Hill next to St. Margaret Patten's church parsonage'.

The HEN AND CHICKEN'S LANE in Walworth, a few years back, is now part of Alvey Street, and originally ran from Park Place across EAST LANE (now East Street) to King (now Kinglake) Street, next to Surrey Square. A public-house preserves the old name at No. 54. This East Lane ran from about 275 Walworth Road (opposite what is now called Penrose Street, and was then WEST LANE) to Old Kent Road. A West Lane at one time ran from Monmouth Street (demolished in forming Shaftesbury Avenue and Cambridge Circus) to ST. MARTIN'S LANE, forming a corner with Lichfield Street. The part which remains is now called West Street.

Part of Little Britain, once Duke Street, was previously named DUCK LANE, then a noted place for old books, booksellers and publishers. This was a great haunt of Pepys: In March, 1668, 'To Duck Lane and there bought Montaigne's *Essays in English*'. In April of the same year, he was again attracted and though he says he bought *Legend* he 'there kissed bookseller's wife'! In July he says he 'walked to Duck Lane and there to the bookseller's at the Bible. I did there look upon and try some books, and made way for coming again to the man.' No mention of any woman here.

The Bible was probably the sign of the 'Hand and Bible', where in 1641 one of Lord Brooke's productions was published. Another publisher's sign in this lane was the 'Angel', at which house was printed *The Famous History of Friar Bacon*: 'Very Pleasant and Delightful to the End', for

W. Thackery. Then there were the 'Bell' (1671, W. White-wood) and the 'Black Raven' (J. Conyers).

In *A View of Sundry Examples, etc.*, imprinted at London for William Wright about 1580, we learn that in Duck Lane in 1575 lived a certain widow who went to the house of one Richard Williamson in Wood Street, whose wife used to dress Flax and Tow, and took six pounds of Tow, and departed without paying therefor.

A Duck Lane is still in existence in Edward Street, Soho, off Wardour Street.

Another Duck Lane, swept away about 1845 for Westminster improvements, comprised part of the Rookery which then existed in the district between Great Smith and Victoria Streets.

DUCK's FOOT LANE—Upper Thames Street to Lawrence Pountney Hill—is properly DUKE's FOOT-LANE, from the Dukes of Suffolk who lived at the Manor of the Rose in the parish of St. Lawrence Pountney. This lane was probably the Duke's foot-lane, or narrow way to and from his mansion. Shakespeare referred to this Manor in his *King Henry VIII*, when Buckingham's Surveyor tells the King—

> Not long before your Highness sped to France
> The Duke, being at the Rose, within the parish
> St. Laurence Poulteney, did of me demand
> What was the speech among the Londoners
> Concerning the French journey

—wishing to impeach his master. DUXFORD LANE is given by Dodsley. Perhaps this was it.

In SUFFOLK LANE, Upper Thames Street, was the entrance to the old site of Merchant Taylor's School. This Company purchased in 1561 part of Sussex House, includ-

Long Lane, Smithfield.

ing a Gate house, a long court, a winding stair leading to leads over the chapel, two galleries at the south end of the court, and part of the chapel. In 1860 the Company bought the remainder of the mansion and site of the garden for £20,000 in order to enlarge the school, which remained here until 1874. Ninety thousand pounds was spent on acquiring a large portion of Charterhouse in 1873.

Suffolk Lane is the next lane west of old Ducksfoot Lane, which latter is now called Laurence Pountney Hill, and runs from Laurence Pountney Hill to 151 Upper Thames Street.

The lane took its name from the noble family of Suffolk (de la Pole), who anciently had property on this spot—the Manor of the Rose already mentioned.

Besides Ducksfoot Lane, Laurence Pountney Hill had another name. In Noorthouck's map of 1772 it is called BURFORD LANE. In trying to trace this name I find that Thomas Romayn, a pepperer and Mayor in 1309–10, left to his daughter Roesia and to John de Burford, her husband, certain rents in the parish of Aldermariecherche.

In 1329 Roesia de Barford [*sic*], her husband being dead, left goods and chattels to her son James and her daughter Katherine to remain in the hands of John de Poltenaye as their guardian. This John de Poltenaye became four times Lord Mayor and was knighted, being a member of the Draper's Company and Alderman of Farringdon Ward. He was buried in St. Paul's Church.

The upper part of St. Laurence Pountney Hill was called, until 1819, GREEN LETTUCE LANE, a corruption of GREEN LATTICE LANE from the lattice gate which opened from the garden of the mansion into what is now Cannon Street.

J. Roberts in his *New Review of London*, 1728, mentions a

Green Nutter's Lane in Cannon Street. Is this a still further corruption of Green Lattice Lane?

Laurence Pountney Lane was of course Laurence Poultney Lane. At the beginning of 1543 Master Arundel kept a house of entertainment here, much resorted to by gay young men of that time. Henry, Earl of Surrey (the poet), was summoned before the Privy Council to answer certain charges. Mistress Arundel, being examined, seems to have given them all away, saying they ate meat in Lent and committed other improprieties, amongst which was that of using stone bows to shoot 'at the queens on the Bankside' while rowing on the Thames at night.

Lawrence Lane runs off Cheapside to Gresham Street.

Before the Fire of London this lane and Ironmonger Lane were the only accesses to the Guildhall from Cheapside until land was bought and King Street was formed.

The famous Blossom's, corruptly Bosom's Inn, was in Lawrence Lane according to an old cab-fares list, exactly 25 poles from Cheapside—and had as a sign St. Lawrence the Deacon in a border of blossoms or flowers. In 1522, when Charles V came over, this was one of the inns set apart for his retinue. 'XX beddes and a stable for IX horses' were directed to be got ready for him.

This inn was entirely destroyed in the Great Fire, but was rebuilt. The Yard is now a depot for receiving goods for despatch by rail. Herbert de Winton mentions the lane of St. Lawrence de Candlewystrate in his Will in 1282.

Allen mentions a Laurence Lane as being in Princes Liberty Lambeth, in 1828, in New Street. The old Lawrence Lane in High Street, St. Giles's, is now Lawrence Street.

CHAPTER II

ODSLEY GIVES US FIVE COW LANES. I HAVE DIS-covered six as well as COW CROSS LANE, which is now Cowcross Street, and the only one preserving the name of Cow. One of these so-named lanes is now King Street, West Smithfield. This lane was mentioned in Ben Jonson's *Bartholomew Fair*—'Sir, my mother has had her nativity cast by the cunning-men in Cow Lane'—then a great place for booksellers and coach-makers. Our old garrulous gossip Pepys visited the latter establishments here, and though he found a carriage 'which did please him mightily' for £50, and his wife so that 'she was almost out of herself for joy almost', yet a friend found 'most infinite fault with it'.

When Dr. Johnson was asked by Mrs. Thrale how he liked the little Miss, and was she fine enough, he replied in his usual courteous manner: 'It was the finery of a beggar, and you know it was: she looked like a native of Cow Lane dressed up to be carried to Bartholomew Fair!'

The passage to the famous George Inn in Snow Hill was through Cow Lane, which lane was built over the site of the ancient gallows. The old house of the Prior of Semper-ingham was here.

Another lane of this name (680 yards in length), together with ARTICHOKE LANE just south of it, was demolished in the formation of the West London Docks; a third (440 yards long) off NEW GRAVEL LANE, in the making of the East London Docks. A fourth was off Lower Queen Street, Trinity Street, Rotherhithe Old Road. Yet another at Stepney Green; while the last was a turning off Liquor Pond Street (which street is now swallowed up by Clerkenwell Road).

'Cow Cross Lane' (now Cowcross Street) 'on the left-hand side of St. John Street . . . of a cross some time standing there; which lane turneth down to another lane called Turnmill Street.' There was a RED COW LANE at Hammersmith mentioned in the Post Office list of principal streets, etc., 1857.

I suppose for number CROSS LANES head the list. Dodsley gives ten. I have only been able to trace nine:

One at St. Mary at Hill, the second turning on the left going towards the river; a second down St. Dunstan's Hill, the second turning on the left into HARP LANE. Another, given in Large's *Way about London*, was through Newton Street, Holborn, to Cross Lane. There are only two turnings there now on the west side, Macklin Street and Parker Street; with Kennedy Court on the east.

That part of the present Lupus Street, Pimlico, which ran from BAKER'S LANE (now Sutherland Street) to Ranelagh Road, was called Cross Lane.

A Cross Lane is given by Cary as being in Long Acre and as 20 poles in length. One hundred and ten yards is a good distance. It is marked in a map of 1773. Starts nearly opposite—a little east—to James Street—made almost a junction with Earl Street in Castle Street. Must be the old name for present Neal Street. BUSH LANE, Cannon Street, has a Cross Lane on its east side.

Another at Shad Thames ran from there by the Dockhead to Thomas Street. It is now incorporated in Queen Elizabeth Street.

An eighth off LOVE LANE, Eastcheap.

The last off Marigold Street, Rotherhithe Wall.

CROSSFIELD LANE runs from High Street, Deptford, to Church Street.

Bush Lane, Cannon Street, immediately east of the railway station, was once famous for needles. Lenton in his *Characterisme or Leisures*, 1631, has: 'And now they may go look for this Bush Lane needle in a bottle of hay.' Noorthouck tells us that about the middle of the street now (1772) called Bush Lane, the Roman General after his first landing on this side, pitched his tent, which was paved, as was customary among the Roman Generals, and was encompassed about by the soldiers, both horse and foot. This pavement was dug up some time after the Great Fire, and part of it was placed in the Museum of the Royal Society.

In the catalogue of exhibits of topographical drawings and prints, at the opening of the new Library and Museum of the Corporation of London in 1872, is mentioned a pencil view by T. Shepherd, 1852, of the exterior of Plumbers' Hall in Bush Lane. This belonged to the Gardner Collection.

Stow says: 'Next to this great house (the Erber) is a lane turning to Bush Lane (of old time called CARTER'S LANE, of carts and carmen having stables there), and now called CHEQUER LANE, or Alley, off an inn called The Chequer.'

LITTLE BUSH LANE is off Bush Lane. In the Post Office

List for 1857, a GREAT BUSH LANE is mentioned. This was probably the present Bush Lane. Plumber's Hall was in Great Bush Lane. The Company was incorporated by James I, and is thirty-first in station of the Livery Companies of London.

Just east of Bush Lane is SHERBORNE LANE, from King William Street to Abchurch Yard. Stow's explanation of its name is charming. He says a long bourne of sweet water ran down Fenchurch Street and Lombard Street to the west end of St. Mary Woolnoth's Church, where, turning south and breaking into small shares, rills or streams, it left the name of SHARE-BORNE LANE or SOUTHBORNE LANE because it ran south to the river of Thames.

Wheatley suggests that SCIRE-BURN (*scir* = a share, *sciran* = to divide) is the more likely etymology. But in 1272 an assignment of an annual rent for four houses in SHITTEBORWELANE was made by Laurence, son of Humphrey Duket; in 1300 Peter de Brankinge left to his daughter houses in the parish of St. Mary de Abchurch in a lane called SHITEBURUELANE; and in 1303 Robert le Wodere or Weyder (dealer in woad, the dye of the ancient Britons) left a shop in SHITEBURLANE to John le Blake; added to which in the Cromwell Parliament's journal it is mentioned that Robert le Yonge, in his will of 1331, spelled it SHITEBOURNE. It is possible that, since many of the old names spelled the origin of the lanes, there may be some analogy in naming this with Dunghill Lane and Midden Lane, already referred to. Meard Street, Soho, described in my *London Alleys, Byways, and Courts*, seems to belong to the same category.

Thomas Maiden, a Sherborne Lane printer, saved the

London Stone from being destroyed. This in Stow's time was on the south side of Cannon Street. It was removed to the north side close to the wall and south-west door of St. Swithin's Church. On both occasions it was complained of as an obstruction and a nuisance until, by the above-named gentleman's efforts, it was placed in its present position in the wall of St. Swithin's Church.

A couple of years ago, the wheel of a coal-delivery cart, owing to a subsidence of the subsoil, burst the concrete surface of the road by the back entrance of the City Carlton Club (which entrance is in this lane) and sank up to its hub within a few feet of a drain.

In digging foundations for the present church of St. Mary Woolnoth in 1716, many Roman earthen vessels, a considerable number of tusks and bones of boars and goats (probably the Temple of Concord mentioned by the Romans was near here), several medals and bits of metal, tessellated work, part of an aqueduct and a well full of dirt were discovered.

Thos. Withering, the Postmaster to Charles I, fixed his receiving house in this lane in 1637, and lived here.

Nearly opposite Bush Lane in Cannon Street runs ST. SWITHIN'S LANE, at the corner of which stands the parish church dedicated to St. Swithin, a Bishop of Winchester, chancellor to King Egbert, and who died in 806. Dryden, the poet, was married here to the Lady Elizabeth Howard. Salter's Hall and Founder's Hall are both in this lane.

Next eastwards of Sherborne Lane is ABCHURCH LANE, in which Londoners were first to taste French cookery at Pontack's eating-house, called the 'Pontac Head', after the proprietor's father, who was President of the Parliament

D

of Bordeaux; the portrait of whose head served as the signboard. This was the portrait introduced in Plate III of the *Rake's Progress*, as having been put up in place of that of Julius Cæsar. Here were to be tasted the best ragoûts and sauces in London. Swift wrote to Mrs. Dingley: ''Tis odd that this very day (Jany. 26, 1713) Lord Somers, Wharton, Somerset, Halifax, and the whole club of Whig Lords, dined at Pontacks in the City, as I received private notice, they have some damned design.'

The celebrated 'Mother Wells's' cakes and pastries mentioned in Webster's *Northward Ho* were sold in this lane. This lane is named after St. Mary de Abbechirche—the old church was destroyed in the Great Fire. The new one, built by Wren, serves as well for the parish of St. Laurence Poultney. The right of presentation for both parishes belongs to Corpus Christi College, Cambridge.

Stow says he had seen it named Upchurch from standing on rising ground.

Pope acclaims the lane as having contained the dwelling-place of John Moore, inventor of the celebrated worm-powder!

> Oh learned friend of Abchurch Lane
> Who sett'st our entrails free!
> Vain is thy art, thy powder vain,
> Since worms shall e'en eat thee.

NICHOLAS LANE is a few yards east of the last named. It took its name from the church of St. Nicholas Acon, destroyed in the Great Fire and not rebuilt. The emblem of St. Nicholas (patron saint of citizens, merchants and mariners) is three purses of gold, or three golden balls. Hence the arms of the Lombard merchants who settled in

London (now represented by the London Bankers) and the three golden spheres of the present-day pawnbrokers. At the south-west corner of this lane, during excavations made for foundations for the proposed new street (King William Street), several beautiful fragments of Samian ware, some antique rugs and some small lamps were found among old foundations on the Roman level. ASULA FECIT was stamped on the bottom of one lamp. A few years later a large slab inscribed NVM PROV BRITA was found among ruins of a Roman edifice, at eleven feet deep, in the lane. In 1258 Felicia la Colnere left a house here to Richard Fitz Sigar. He left it to Geoffrey le Scinturer (maker of girdles) and his wife.

MARTIN'S LANE, which runs from Cannon Street to Arthur Street, was once called—in the third of Edward I, i.e. 1275—Street of St. Martin Orgor. In the *Calendar of Wills, Court of Husting*, Lane of St. Martin Orgar—1314–15, St. Martin's Lane by Stow, and Martin's Lane in the Ordnance Survey Map 1848–51.

Until about 1831 it extended south to Upper Thames Street. Then the southern end was demolished for foundations of Arthur Street West. Some houses at the northern end have been destroyed for the widening of Cannon Street.

The lane was much in favour with solicitors and wine-merchants. Richard Glover, son of a Hamburgh merchant, and author of *Leonidas*, was born here in 1712. Ordgarus was the founder of St. Martin Orgar Church, burnt in the Great Fire. The remains being found capable of repair, the French Protestants in communion with the Episcopal Church of England obtained a lease of the Tower, got it confirmed by Parliament and have erected a church for their own use.

CROOKED LANE is but a part of what it was when it was so called because of the crooked windings thereof. It now extends but from Arthur Street to 32 King William Street. The rest was demolished in the making of King William Street and the approaches to the new London Bridge. In a record dated 1303, this lane was referred to as 'VENELLA TORTA', and in 1310 as 'LA CROKEDELANE'. A tenement called 'Welhouse in Crokedlan' was mentioned in 1344, and seventy years later the 'east corner of the lane of Crokedlane' was said to be one of the boundaries of the Butcher's Market in Eastcheap.

The lane was long famous for bird-cage and fishing tackle shops. One of the latter—Eaton & Dellers—still remains. Punt fishing for roach off the starlings of London Bridge was a common amusement for city people in the early part of the eighteenth century. The 'Swan in Crooked Lane possessed of strangers, and selling of Rhenish wine' is mentioned by Stow as being one of the most ancient houses in this lane—called the Leaden Porch, and belonged some-time to Sir John Merston, Knight, in the fifteenth century.

An advertisement, 25 May, 1694, states that at one, Mr. Packer's in Crooked Lane, next the Dolphin, are very good lodgings to be let, where there is 'freedom from Noise and a pretty Garden'.

Ben Jonson in his Masque of Christmas has:—

> Last Baby-cake, that an end doth make
> Of Christmas' merry, merry vein-a
> Is Child Rowlan, and a straight young man
> Though he came out of Crooked-Lane-a.

St. Michael's Church, in which Sir William Walworth was buried, was pulled down nearly a century ago. The last Divine Service there was held on Sunday, 20 March, 1831. It was damaged in a curious way on one occasion. Stow says in 1560 on 5 July:

a certain man came into this lane to buy a gun or two, and shooting off a piece, it burst in pieces, went through the house, and spoiled about five houses more; and of that goodly church adjoining it threw down a great part of one side, and left never a glass window whole [the 'w' is not superfluous here]. And by it eight men and one maid were slain and divers hurt.

Some gun and some ammunition to be trying in a shop!

In the *New View of London*, published in 1708, is mentioned a Crooked Lane within the compass of the Mint in Southwark as being one of many places of privilege. This Mint was on the west side of Blackman Street, near against St. George's Church, and in that parish, and was kept at a sumptuous house built by Charles Brandon, Duke of Suffolk, in the reign of Henry VIII, which coming into the King's hands was called Southwork [*sic*] Place and a Mint of coinage was there kept for the King.

From Arthur Street, mentioned above, to 130 Upper Thames Street, runs MILES LANE, at the bottom of some ten steps from Crooked Lane. The earliest mention of this lane in its present form was in the *London Guide* of 1758. In 1277 it was known as the LANE OF ST. MICHAEL DE CANDEL-EVIESTRATE, in 1303 it became SEINT MICHELESLANE; in 1314 the LANE OF ST. MICHAEL DE CROKED LANE, and in 1567 ST. MIGHELLS LANE. It was, of course, named after St. Michael's Church, and the present name is an easy and shortened corruption. It is much altered since I sketched it for my *London Alleys, Byways, and Courts*. There is a very good sketch of it in its old stage made by one of the Mr. Cuddefords (the wine merchants) in their office there, where they have other good things. I have tried some. So I know! This lane also was shortened in making the approach to London Bridge. Previously it was, according to Cary, 31 poles in length.

The custom of causing a bellman, at nights, to go through streets and lanes ringing a bell, crying rhymes suitable to festivals and seasons of the year, and crying 'Hang out your lanterns', is said to have originated in the reign of Queen Mary in January, 1556, and was first practised in Cordwainer Street (the old name for the upper end of Bow Lane) by Alderman Draper. Over a hundred years later one John Cooke, by his will, gave to the churchwardens, etc., of St. Michael's, Crooked Lane, £76 to be laid out to the most profit and advantage for various uses; amongst them for maintenance of a lantern and candle, to be 8 to the lb. at least, to be kept and hanged out at the corner of St. Michael's lane, next Thames Street, from Michaelmas to Lady Day between the hours of 9 and 10 p.m. until 4 or 5 a.m. for affording light to passengers going through Thames Street or St. Michael's Lane.

The famous Boar's Head Tavern mentioned in the time of Richard II, the scene of Falstaff's revels in Shakespeare's *Henry IV*, stood between the end of St. Michael's Lane and Small Alley, the spot having been very nearly that of the present statue of William IV. It was demolished in 1831. The carved stone sign, with date 1668, is preserved in the Guildhall Museum.

Burridge in 1722 gives a KISSER LANE, by Michael's Lane, near Thames Street.

CLEMENT'S LANE, from Lombard Street to King William Street, was named after the Church of St. Clement's in Eastcheap, destroyed in the Great Fire and rebuilt by Sir Christopher Wren. Bishop Pearson was rector of the old church, in which he preached his well-known sermons upon the Creed—which led to his exposition—a standard book in English Divinity. Joseph Ames, the antiquary, died of a fit of coughing in a counting-house belonging to Mr. Ingham Foster here. Rogers, the poet, was for forty years, or more, partner in a banking-house in this lane.

Clement's Lane, Strand, is the western boundary of the land which was destined to be the site for the Law Courts. The lane was once entered from the Strand through an open gateway flanked by massive stone pillars. This was erected by the Corporation of London as a tribute to Alderman Pickett, whose exertions caused the Strand to be widened, at an expense of more than a quarter of a million. The new thoroughfare was then named Pickett Street. The name never took on and the houses were reckoned as part of the Strand.

Once the abode of fashion—the Lords Paget had their town mansion here, Sir John Trevor, Speaker of the House of Commons and twice Master of the Rolls, lived here— the lane became simply a Rookery for the poor Irish of the neighbourhood, and a back slum leading to Clare Market.

About the middle of the lane was an entrance to a large house which had an entrance also into Plough Court. In this house, once used as a poorhouse, no less than eighteen families lived at the same time. Many of the houses—mostly built of a frame-work of wood interlarded with brick and then plastered—were erected in the reigns of James and Elizabeth. One of these was noted as the scenes of royal intrigues which are recounted in the *Memories pour Servir* of Charles II and his Court, in whose time Clement's Lane was the Bond Street of London; where, as Mr. Diprose says,

Steele used to show his gaudy attire, Bolingbroke his stately presence, and Pope that decrepit form which was yet the tabernacle of a noble soul within. Here Swift, with downcast head and scowling visage, used to growl to himself as the mighty satirist made and unmade cabinets; and the gentle Addison here turned some of those polished periods which have called forth the envy and admiration of after ages.

Such are the changes which took place in Clement's Lane.

It was suggested by Moser that here stood an inn as far back as the time of King Ethelred for receipt of penitents who came to St. Clement's Well; that a religious house was afterwards established from which arose the church. On the west side of the lane was the 'Lamb' or 'Holy Lamb' in which were received the guests. The monastery was converted into an inn of the law.

In the confession of Thomas Winter he states that the Gunpowder Plot conspirators met in Clement's Lane behind the church. In his own words:

So we met behind St. Clement's, Mr. Catesby, Mr. Percy, Mr. Wright, Mr. Guy Fawkes, and myself, and, having upon a primer, given each other the oath of secrecy, in a chamber where no other body was, we went after into the next room, and heard mass, and received the blessed sacrament upon the same.

The only part now remaining of CLEMENT's LANE, Strand, is between King's College Hospital and New Inn. Of old it was a long winding lane coming out of old Butcher's Row and fronting Clement's Inn; then, passing by St. Clement's and Boswell Courts (long since demolished), ran northwards into Clare Market, in its passage taking in St. Clement's pump or well, of note for its excellent spring water.

Dugdale says Clement's Inn was an Inn of Chancery in the reign of Edward II. Pennant says it dates back only as far as the reign of Edward IV.

New Inn, built here on the site of a hostelry known as the 'Blessed Virgin', was removed from Seacole Lane and also called Our Ladye Inne. Pennant, in 1805, says the students of the Strand Inn nestled there after they were routed by the Duke of Somerset.

Sir Thomas More received his education here before removing to Lincoln's Inn.

In the State Papers for 1605, 7 November, is the information that Guido Fawkes lodged two months ago with Mrs. Herbert, now Mrs. Wodehouse, at the back of St. Clement's Church.

Nearly opposite Clement's Lane, the other side of Lombard Street, is BIRCHIN LANE. The changes in the spelling of the name of this lane are many. In 1190 it was known as BERCHERUERELANE; in 1260 BERCHERVERES-LANE; in 1320 BERCHERUERELANE; in 1332 BERCHERESLANE; in 1345 BERCHERNER'S LANE; in 1346 BERCHEVERLANE; in 1361 BERCHERUERISLANE; in 1372 BERCHERLANE; in 1386

BIRCHENLANE; in 1393 BIRCHEYN LANE; in 1401 BYRCHERS-
LANE; in 1439 BIRCHERLANE; in 1602 BYRCHYN LANE;
in 1618 BURCHEN LANE; BIRCHOVERIS LANE.

Stow says the right name was 'BURCHEOVER LANE after
Birchover [*sic*], the first builder and owner thereof, now
corruptly called Birchin, and that this lane and the high
street near adjoining hath been inhabited for the most
part with wealthy drapers'.

As early as 1260 one Thomas Travers in his will left to
Sir Geoffrey de Winton his land in Berchervereslane.
According to Anderson, in 1372 (during the reign of
Edward III) at least twenty houses in Birchin Lane—in
the very heart of the city—came under the denomination
of cottages, and were so conveyed to St. Thomas's Hospital
in Southwark. The shops, as drawn in Aggas's map of
London, appear to have been detached and separate
tenements, or at least unconnected with houses, the shops
being known by the signs attached.

Major Gaunt, author of *The Observations on the Bills of
Mortality*, lived in this lane.

The well-known Tom's Coffee House was here, the
rendezvous of young city merchants at Change time.

Middleton's *Black Book* (1604) has: 'And passing through
Birchin Lane, amidst a camp-royal of hose and doublets,
I took excellent occasion to slip into a captain's suit, a
valiant buff doublett stuffed with points and a pair of
velvet slops scored thick with lace.'

In *The Return from Parnassus* (1606) we read: 'And you,
master Amoretto . . . it's fine, when that puppet-player,
Fortune, must put such a Birchin Lane post in so good
a suit—such an ass is so good fortune.'

Dekker's *Gull's Hornbrook* (1609) gives us: 'Did many think you come wrangling into the world about no better matters, than all his lifetime to make privy searches in Birchin Lane for whalebone doublets?'

Strype says the lane was a place of considerable trade, especially for men's apparel. As early as the end of the sixteenth century it was a great mart for ready-made clothes.

> No sooner in London will we be,
> But the bakers for you, the brewers for me.
> Birchin Lane will *suit us*,
> The costermongers fruit us.

In 1345, one Byndo, a Lombard, of Florence, was taken at the suit of John de Croydone, servant of John atte Bell, vintner, with the mainour of six silver cups and half of a broken cup stolen in Bercherner's Lane (yet another spelling) in the Ward of Langebourne in London. 'The jury say upon their oath, that the said Byndo was guilty of the felony aforesaid. Therefore he is to be hanged.'

Ascham speaks of a common proverb of this lane. To send a person to Birching Lane has an obvious meaning; and to return to Weeping Cross was a joke of kindred origin.

Advertisement. 26 July, 1695.

At the Marine Coffee House in Birchin Lane is water-gruel to be sold every morning from six till eleven of the clock. 'Tis not yet thoroughly known, but there comes such a company as drinks usually four or five gallons in a morning.

Zachary Macaulay and his infant son, afterwards the historian, lived in a house in this lane, where The Sierra

Leone Company had its office. Zachary was secretary to that Company.

In Lombard Street was the parish church of St. Nicholas Acon, or Hacon. S. NICHOLAS HAKOUN LANE is mentioned in Roger de Kanefeud's will in 1297. This must be the same as the present Nicholas Lane.

FINCH LANE is practically a continuation, the other side of Cornhill, of Birchin Lane. Named after Robert Finke, his son of the same name, James Finke and Rosamond Finke. 'The elder new built church of St. Benet, commonly called Finke of the founder' as Stow has it.

It is curious that, as has been said previously, Fynkeslane, according to a will dated 1452, was an early name of Pudding Lane.

'Joe's' here was long famous for its mutton-chops.

The freehold of the Cock and Woolpack Tavern, in the lane, was sold in 1872 at Garraway's for £20,000. John de Honylane, in 1274, left to Cristina, his wife, his houses upon Cornhill at the corner of Fynkeslane for life. In 1293 an earthen wall belonging to William and Gilbert de Asshindone in FYNKIS LANE was presented as a nuisance. A bequest of rents in FYNGHIS LANE was made to the church of St. Benedict Fyng by John de Wrytele, carpenter, in 1305.

James Watt, in 1765, was working in Finch Lane with an instrument maker, John Morgan, who taught him to be proficient in making theodolites, quadrants, compasses, etc.

Just across Threadneedle Street, running through to Lothbury on the east side of the Bank of England, is BARTHOLOMEW LANE, called so after the church of that

name taken down in 1841 when the then new Royal
Exchange was built by Sir William Tite. Capel Court
here forms one entrance to the Stock Exchange. Stow
says the most ancient house here was the Bishop of St.
Albans'. A once-famous Auction Mart (now covered by a
large block of offices) stood here. One of the most bland
and fascinating-mannered auctioneers who ever wielded
an ivory hammer—Mr. George Robins—was the pre-
siding genius. His notice of the sale of the selling of the
old Olympic Theatre, at which was the popular Madame
Vestris, was a masterpiece of allurement and adroitness.
Having got the bidding to £3,400, he was allowing his
hammer slowly to descend with 'Going—going—go—'
when the highest bidder exclaimed 'The Theatre is mine!'
Mr. Robins stopped suddenly and remarked that he
didn't in the least wonder that the bidder's anxiety to
possess the theatre at such a figure should cause him to
anticipate his decision, declared that the property was
still in the market, thus giving bidders one more chance
of making their fortunes without risk or trouble, and
eventually sold it for £5,850.

St. Bartholomew-the-Less Lane is mentioned in the
wills of John de Littlestone, clerk, in 1300, and of Geoffrey
Fayrher, cook, in 1348, each of them bequeathing tenements therein.

Robert de Norhampton left to his wife Margery tenements in Slapereslane in the parish of St. Bartholomew-
the-Less in 1316.

The continuation westward of Lothbury is now Gresham
Street. This is made up, since 1845, of the old Cateaton
Street, Lad Lane, Maiden Lane and St. Ann's Lane.

The former extended from Lothbury to Aldermanbury; Lad Lane from there to Wood Street; Maiden Lane thence to Foster Lane, and St. Ann's Lane on to St. Martin's-le-Grand. This St. Ann's Lane was previously called POPE LANE, according to Hughson, from an ancient proprietor of that name, opposite to the churchyard of St. John Zachary. St. Anne's Church here was known as St. Anne in the Willows, on account of the trees in the churchyard.

Stow says this lane lay on the north of this church, and was mentioned in the Harleian MSS., certain tenements being described as temp. Edward I.

Another St. Ann's Lane was at 30 Great Peter Street, Westminster. This was named from the Chapel of the Mother of Our Lady, and was built upon part of the orchard and fruit gardens of the Abbey. Henry Purcell and Dr. Heather, the famous musicians, lived here; also Herrick, the poet, when ejected from his living of Dean Prior.

Sir Roger de Coverley, when a stripling, had occasion to inquire the way to this St. Ann's Lane, and was promptly called a young Popish cur, and asked who had made Ann a saint! The next person he met of whom he inquired called him a prick-eared cur, and told him that she had been a saint before he was born, and would be a saint after he was hanged, instead of answering his question. Then, he says, he went into every lane in the district asking what it was called, and by adopting this artifice found the place.

St. Martin's-le-Grand was known as St. Martin's Lane before the rebuilding of the city after the Great Fire. It was the principal street of the liberty of St. Martin's-le-Grand and noted for its shops for the sale of imitation jewellery, etc.

In this lane of old time was a large college of a dean and secular canons or priests founded by two brothers Ingelricus and Edwardus in 1056, and confirmed by William the Conqueror in 1068. This college claimed great privileges of sanctuary and otherwise. It was surrendered to Edward V, 1548, in which year the college church was pulled down. On the east part thereof was built a large tavern and many large houses. On the west side of the Lane, towards Aldersgate, stood Northumberland House, the City mansion of Earl Percy in Henry IV's time. Henry gave it to his wife, Queen Jane, as her wardrobe. It afterwards became a printing house.

In Lad Lane was the famous carrier's inn, 'The Swan with Two Necks', whence passengers and goods were despatched to the north for over a century and a half.

> True sportsmen know no dread nor fear,
> Each rides when once the saddle in,
> As if he had a neck to spare,
> Just like the Swan in Ladlane—

is a couplet from the Huddersfield Cape Hunt. As Camden Hotten facetiously puts it—notwithstanding the 'double bill' suggested by the two heads, it still continued a favourite sign.

A record of 1301 mentions LADELANE, referring to a house situate there belonging to 'Coke Bateman the Jew'. Lad Lane was recorded as LADLE LANE in the parish records of St. Michael, Wood Street, according to Stow; who says the above-mentioned Maiden Lane was called, of old time, INGGELANELANE, ENGAIN, INGENE or ING LANE, but gives no reasons. At the north-west corner, and against Goldsmith's Hall, stood the before-mentioned parish church of St. John Zachary. In a will dated 1310, of Agnes la Bret, is bequeathed a messuage in the parish of St. John Zakarie near INGELLENELANE, and in 1331 one Edmund de London, clerk, mentions his houses in ENGLES-LANE, parish of S. Michael de Hoggenelane.

From Gresham Street, at its west end, FOSTER LANE runs to 147 Cheapside. This lane in olden times was inhabited chiefly by Goldsmiths. The Hall of their Company is at the Gresham Street end, the site of which was bought by them, in 1323, with tenements. The assay possessed by this Company compels every article of manufacturers in gold or silver to be marked with the 'Hall Mark' before it leaves the workman's hands, and authorizes the Wardens to break whatever article is below standard.

In 1271 this lane was mentioned as 'SEINT UASTES LANE, qui ducit versus Aldridesgate'. In its early days it extended further north and included Noble Street. Nearly the whole of one side was demolished between 1824 and 1825 for the, then, New Post Office. Just by Cheapside, in the lane, in the seventeenth century, stood the old Dagger Tavern, famous for its pies. These were often referred to in plays of the time.

'I'll not take thy word for a dagger pie' occurs in one of Dekker's plays.

Prynne, in one of his, has—'And please you, let there be dagger pies.'

They were, I believe, mince-pies.

St. Vedast Church was one of the fifty new churches

Foster Lane, Cheapside.

built in London by Sir Christopher Wren, according to
Mr. Joseph Ames, F.R.S. The old one was dedicated to
St. Vedast, Bishop of Arras, says Maitland; and that the
first time he found it mentioned in history was 'that Walter
de London was presented there in 1308'. It was not
entirely destroyed by the Great Fire, though nothing was
left standing but the walls. The crazy steeple continued
standing until 1694 when it was taken down and beautifully rebuilt at the charge of the united parishes of this and
St. Michael Quern.

An interesting and curious stone coffin is preserved in a
vault under a small brick grave on the north side of the
church. It was found in 1831 by some workmen who were
digging a drain opposite No. 17 Cheapside. It then contained a skeleton.

Robert Herrick, who was born in Cheapside in 1591,
was baptized in the old St. Vedast's.

John Massingham, of the Middle Temple, in his diary
—date 19 December, 1602—relates that having with many
heard a sermon 'at Paules from one with a long brown
beard, a hanging look, a gloting eye, and a toosing learing
jesture', went to hear at St. Vedast's 'one Clappam, a
black fellowe with a sowere look but a good spirit, bold,
and sometimes bluntly witty; his text, Solomon's Song—
Thy lips are like a thread of skarlett. . . . There are
enough of Rahab's profession in every place. . . . I would
not give a penny for an hundred of them,' said he.

Upon the west side of the lane stood the small parish
church of St. Leonard, which, Stow tells us, was enlarged
and repaired about the year 1631. Part of the Post Office
—now itself demolished, and huge blocks of offices erected

E

upon its site—was built on the site of this old church, destroyed in the Great Fire.

Paternoster Row, called Paternosterstrete in 1312, was known as PATERNOSTER LANE in 1321, and finally as Paternostersrowe in 1349. Stow says it was so called

because of stationers, or textwriters that dwelt there, who wrote and sold all sorts of books then in use, namely A.B.C. with the Pater Noster, Ave, Creed, Graces, etc. There dwelt also Turners of beads, and they were called Pater Noster makers, as I read in a record of one Robert Nikke, Pater Noster maker, and citizen, in the reign of Henry IV, and so of others.

He goes on to explain:

At the end of Pater Noster Row is Ave Mary Lane, so called upon the like occasion of text writers and bead makers then dwelling there, and at the end of that lane is likewise CREEDE LANE, late so called, but some time Spurrier Row, of spurriers dwelling there; and Amen Lane is added there into betwixt the south end of Warwicke Lane and the north end of Ave Mary Lane.

Anent these lanes Mr. John Parry in the *Gentleman's Magazine* for 1828, Part I, page 213, ingeniously suggests as an origin for the names a Romish procession on Corpus Christi Day, or Holy Thursday:

Let us suppose processioners mustered and marshalled at upper end of Paternoster Row next Cheapside. These commence to march westward, and begin to chant the Pater Noster, continued this whole length of the street (thence Pater Noster Lane). On arrival at the bottom of the street, they enter Ave Maria Lane, at the same time beginning to chant the Salutation of the Virgin 'Ave Maria', which continues until reaching Ludgate Hill, and crossing over to Creed Lane. They then commence the chant of the 'Credo' which continues until they reach the spot now called Amen Corner, where they sing the concluding 'Amen'.

In connection with AMEN LANE Stow mentions

From the South end of Warwicke Lane to the north end of Ave Mary Lane, there is a short lane which runneth west some small distance, and is there closed up with a gate into a great house; and this is a great house built of stone and timber of old time pertaining to John Duke of Britaine, Earl of Richmond, called Burgavenny House.

Old EXCHANGE LANE is mentioned in the same connection.

The clause 'Commonly called Bishop Bonner's stable' occurring in many of the leases under which several of the houses in AVE MARIA LANE are held, shows the likelihood of that sworn enemy to Protestants having resided here at one time. And, as he is reputed by history to have examined those charged with heresy, and tortured them in his own house, it is quite possible that a number of human bones discovered, in 1806, in a well—a brick-built receptacle covered with an oblong piece of marble about 34 × 16 inches—in a cellar, by the workmen digging for a foundation in order to shore up the wall of a house, may have belonged to some of his victims.

In Paternoster Lane in 1817, Thomas Moore took £3,000 for his *Lalla Rookh* from the firm which had purchased the business of the publisher of *Robinson Crusoe* nearly a century earlier, at the old sign of 'The Ship and Black Swan'.

At the sign, boldly carved in wood, of the 'Bible and Crown', coloured and gilt, in the stringcourse above the window, were the High Church Publishers, the Rivingstons, from 1710–1853, where they contained the Annual Register which belonged to Dodsley of Pall Mall. The *London Magazine* was published at No. 47, in 1732, by Robert Baldwin, before the noted Edinburgh firm had the premises.

The famous old Chapter Coffee House (closed as such in 1853) had been for more than a century the resort of literary men, publishers and booksellers. Stow mentions another Paternoster Lane. Describing the places in Vintry Ward, having given all on the Thames side, he says: 'On the land side is the Royall Street and Paternoster Lane, I think of old time called Arches'. He mentions that he read that Robert de Suffolke gave to Walter Darford his tenement with the appurtenance in the lane called LES ARCHES, in the parish of St. Michael de Paternoster Church.

Off the now-named Paternoster Row, at No. 22 is IVY LANE. Stow's description of this lane is: 'Next to Ivie Lane, so called of ivy growing on the walls of the prebend houses; but now the lane is replenished on both sides with faire houses, and divers offices be there kept by registers,' etc. The north-east corner has been demolished and rebuilt just lately.

The lane was here *temp.* Henry III; for it was then spelled IVILANE and inhabited by chandlers who supplied wax tapers for St. Paul's and the City churches. They were threatened with penalties if they made their wykes of excessive weight, so as to be selling wyke for wax; then the 'wicked waxed exceeding' to no purpose. In the index of an old MS. YVIESLANE, alias ALSIESLANE, is given.

FUKEMAR LANE in 1280; FOLKMARES LANE, and in 1285

FOLKMERE LANE—these names arose from the ground set apart for meetings of the Folkmoot on the east of St. Paul's Church where the new burial-ground then was. The lane finally reverted to its old name of Ivy. Richard Royston, 'bookseller to three kings', the publisher's agent, and friend of Jeremy Taylor, had his shop in this lane in the seventeenth century at the sign of the 'Angel'.

Roger L'Estrange had his office, as Licenser of the Press, and for the publishing of the *Intelligencer* at the 'Gun' in Ivy Lane, where in 1663 he was ready to pay 40s. for information of any private printing press, with assurance of secrecy as to the person giving such information.

The Ivy Lane Club created by Dr. Johnson met at the 'King's Head' here, and the Hum-Drum Club mentioned in No. 9 of the *Spectator* also met—and held its silent meetings—in this lane. Addison—he was a member— tells us that it 'was made up of very honest gentlemen, of peaceable dispositions, that used to sit together, smoke their pipes, and say nothing till midnight'. He does not tell us what they said after that hour. It was over a century too soon for Carlyle and Tennyson.

There is another Ivy Lane west of Hoxton Road, off St. John's Road, nearly opposite Nicholas Street.

IVY BRIDGE LANE, or IVE LANE, is in the Strand. Peter Cunningham's direction was 'the first turning west of Salisbury Street, leading to the halfpenny steamboats'. Salisbury Street was demolished in the building of the Cecil Hotel. Of old, Durham House was the most easterly house in the Strand belonging to St. Martin's parish, and Ivy Bridge Lane marked the eastern limit of that parish, and separated Durham House from the Bishop of Carlisle's Inn. Ivie Bridge was in the High Street, and had a way under it leading down to the Thames. The lane parted the liberty of the Duchy from the City of Westminster on that south side.

Old Maiden Lane, in connection with the formation of Gresham Street, has been mentioned. There are now only two lanes of this name in the Post Office directory —one the first on the left up Southampton Street, Strand, the other the third on the left down Garlick Hill, Upper Thames Street; at the south-west end of which is the Church of St. James, Garlickhithe. A curious tale is told of a one time Rector of this church—in 1531—who was made Bishop of Bangor later. He is said to have sold five fair bells out of the steeple of his cathedral; to have gone to the seaside to see them shipped away, and to have been struck with blindness immediately afterwards, so that he never saw again.

The *Post Office List of Principal Streets and Places in London and its Environs* for 1857 gives these two Maiden Lanes and two more—one in Holloway and one at King's Cross. To this latter I have referred as having been probably called Midden Lane—I am not able to trace one at Holloway. Rocque gives one off Half Moon Street, also untraceable by me.

Maiden Lane at King's Cross was the ancient way from Gray's Inn to Highgate, nearly three miles long. It was the boundary road all the way between the parishes of Islington and St. Pancras. Norden calls it LONGWICH LANE, corrupted of LONGHEDGE LANE, by which name it was frequently spoken of. From King's Cross to Camden Road it is now called York Road; thence to Junction Road,

Maiden Lane. W.C.

Kentish Town, Brecknock Road; from there to Highgate Hill, Dartmouth Hill Road. Camden in his *Britannia* says this road was open in 1300. It was 'refused of wayfaring men and carriers by reason of the deepness and dirtie passage in the winter season'. Hence the reason for the road over Highgate Hill on the top of which a toll gate was erected to pay the Bishop of London £40 per annum as the road went through his park.

Maiden Lane, leaving Highgate on the west, passed through TALLINGDONE LANE—it also fell into HAGBUSH LANE. This Tallingdone or TOLENTONE LANE was the afterward-called Du Val's Lane, or Devil's Lane mentioned in connection with long lanes, and is now Hornsey Road. The manor of Tolentone is mentioned in Domesday Book.

Maiden Lane, Southampton Street, Covent Garden, has many literary, stage, and artistic memories.

Isaac D'Israeli in his *Curiosities of Literature* says it was so called from a statue of the Virgin Mary which, in Catholic days, adorned the corner of the street. It is described in the early rate books of St. Paul's, Covent Garden, as 'Maiden Lane, behind the Bull Inn'. Here is still a Bull Inn Court leading to the Strand.

Voltaire, in 1726, lodged at the White Peruke in this lane. In a garret here Andrew Marvell, with only cold mutton for dinner, refused the Lord Treasurer Danby's bribe.

Turner's address, No. 26 (as given in the R.A. Catalogue for 1794), was on the north side nearly opposite the Adelphi stage door. His father was a barber here. House cleared away in the late eighties. Munday's coffee-house was here; also the Cider Cellars—a favourite resort of Porson, Lord Campbell in his early days, and other notable personages. Devilled kidneys, oysters, welsh rarebits, cigars, brandy and large supplies of London stout furnished the cuisine till all disappeared in the extending of the Adelphi Theatre. The new Charing Cross Bridge may demand further changes in this lane. But in spite of all alterations, regulations cannot exist without 'Rules'.

A Maiden Lane was described by Dodsley as extending 'from Deadman's Place to Gravel Lane, a long straggling place with ditches on each side; the passage to the houses being over little bridges'. This was originally called MAID LANE and is now represented by New Park Street, and the portion of Great Guildford Street between Gravel Lane and Sumner Street. The old Globe Theatre stood near Maid Lane, here, on the Bankside 'within 80 paces of the mill which was John Whalley's Windmill', says Chalmers. Malone says it stood *in* Maid Lane. During performances a flag with the Cross of St. George upon it was unfurled from the roof.

The principal prison of the Clink stood at the corner of Maid Lane. It was removed in 1745 to Deadman's Place (so-called from the number buried there during the Great Plague). It was burned down in the 1780 riots.

Great Guildford Street at one time rejoiced in being called Bandy-leg-Walk (distinctly given in 1772 map) and was but a dirty lane out of Maid Lane across Dyer's Field (with a pond in the middle) to Queen Street, which last is now Union Street. This part was the St. Giles of Southwark.

A ROYAL OAK LANE is given by Lockie as being in

Maid Lane, Boro', the first on the left from Park Street
(old Deadman's Place). That would have been just north
of two lanes marked in Noorthouck's 1772 map, DIRTY
LANE and FOUL LANE—leading into the Boro' High
Street. They ran across STONEY and COUNTER LANES
(both Streets now).

A Maid Lane off Church Street, Lambeth, is given by
Thomas Allen, in 1828, in his *History and Antiquities* of that
district. Church Street and its old continuation, Canter-
bury Place, are now swallowed up by Lambeth Road.
In Nicholson's *New View of London*, 1708, a MAIDENHEAD
LANE is given as being on the south side of Great Russell
Street near the west end. I cannot trace this. There were,
commencing from the west end, Dyott Street (as now),
Plumtree Street (now Bloomsbury Street), Vine Street
(now Willoughby Street), and Duke Street (now Coptic
Street). In one old map is an unnamed turning out of
Dyott (or George) Street, north of Bainbridge Street; that
may have been it. Or it may have been completely
demolished among the numbers of tenements and houses,
of which the walls subsided, when the great porter vat—
the talk of London at its construction—burst (about 1814)
owing to the defective state and insecurity of some of its
hoops. The lane may possibly have been taken in to form
the garden of the mansion house on the brewery premises
which had its entrance in Great Russell Street.

One Maidenhead Lane (afterwards called DISTAFF
LANE) was wiped out for the formation of Queen Victoria
Street, which was also the cause of the disappearance of
ST. THOMAS LANE, BASING LANE, PISSING LANE and TURN-
BAS LANE, all named in Aggas's map of 1560. Gerard's

Inn Hall, where the then Lord Mayor of London transacted the city business, was used as a cellar to an inn known by the same name with an entrance by a winding stair of nineteen steps from the yard. Another part of the Hall, down two pair of stairs from Basing Lane, belonged to a Mr. Harvey, glover, in Cornhill. There was also an entrance from the Hall through a narrow brick-arched passage to the burying-vault under Bread Street Church.

According to Stow another lane turned down by the west gate of the Tower Royal—TOWER ROYAL LANE. Strype says this was in Bridge Row (in 1755).

Turnbas Lane—from the west gate of Tower Royal west to Cordwainer Street (the present Bow Lane)—was mentioned in the will, 1328, of Thos. de Evenefeld, pepperer, as TORNEBASTON LANE in the parish of S. Mary de Aldermaricherche.

TURNWHEEL LANE, south out of Cannon Street and south and south-west to Dowgate Hill, was demolished for the erection of Cannon Street Station. The church of St. Mary Bothaw was in this lane before the Great Fire. Stow says it was 'a little lane with a turnepike in the middel thereof'. The church took its name from the boat-haw, or boat-builder's yard in the vicinity.

A ST. MARIE BUTOLPH LANE, continuation of Dowgate Hill to Cannon Street, is marked in the 1560 map.

TURNAGAIN LANE = Turnback (1666 Leake), WINDAGAINE LANE was at the east end out of Snow Hill, demolished for formation of Holborn Viaduct and its approaches. Tindale's words in 1531 are quoted in connection with it —'a Turnagaine lane which they cannot goe through'. Le Coldabbeye in WENDAGEYNESLANE was a tenement

Maid Lane

belonging to the Fraternity of St. Katherine in the Sepulchre's Church in which William de Wyle had a leasehold interest in 1361. In the will of John Hereward, 1308, it is given as WANDAYENESLANE.

There was a Turnagain Lane off Thomas Street, Gainsford Street, HORSLEYDOWN LANE.

Near the first-mentioned Turnagain Lane is SEACOAL LANE, in the turning towards Holborn Conduit in Turnagain Lane; or rather, as in a record of the fifth Edward III: 'Windagain Lane for that it goeth down West to Fleet Dike, from whence men must turn again the same way they came, for there it stopped.' On the east side of Faringdon Street, it is sadly shorn of its ancient proportions. As to its reputation: 'Feby. 28th, 1560. In Turnagayne Lane . . . a lame woman with a knef kylled a proper man.' 'March 8th, 1560. Rode to hanging the woman that killed the man in Turnagayne Lane.' These excerpts are from Machyn's diary.

New Inn is said to have been situate in Seacoal Lane before being removed to Wych Street, where it adjoined Clement's Inn. Stow thinks this lane was originally called LIMEBURNER'S LANE, and that it took its present name from the burning of lime there with sea coal. But in the will of Wm. de Hakeneye, tanner, 27 May, 1339, he bequeathed to his son Michael his tenement in the lane called LYMBRENNERESLANE *near* SECOLLANE in the parish of S. Sepulchre in the suburb of London. So they were two distinct lanes. And long before this—in 1308—I find John Hereward bequeathed to Katherine, his daughter, shops in Secollane *and* LYMBARNERESLANE.

Seacoal Lane on the south side of Skinner Street (now

Holborn Viaduct and approach) contained a steep flight
of steps—called Break-neck Steps—ascending to Green
Arbour Court, in which Court Oliver Goldsmith lived for
some time.

In 1343 Edward III, for the decency and cleanliness of
the city, granted upon lease to the Butchers in the parish
of St. Nicholas Shambles a piece of land in 'Secollane near
to the water of Flete' for the purpose of there in such
water cleansing the entrails of beasts. The butchers were
to repair a certain 'key' [*sic*] there at their own charges,
and keep it in repair. The rent was to be paid to the
Mayor of London for the time being, at the Feast of the
Lord's Nativity, one boar's head.

Swift seems to have had this in mind when he wrote:

> Now from all parts the swelling kennels flow,
> And bear their trophies with them as they go;
> Filths of all hues and odours seem to tell
> What street they sail'd from by their syght and smell.
> They, as each torrent drives, with rapid force,
> From Smithfield to St. Pulchre's shape their course,
> And in huge confluence join'd at Snow Hill ridge,
> Fall from the conduit prone to Holborn Bridge;
> Sweepings from butchers' stalls, dung, guts and blood,
> Drown'd puppies, stinking sprats, all drench'd in mud,
> Dead cats and turnip-tops came tumbling down the flood.

Lord Chesterfield's reply to the enthusiastic Frenchman
who asked him whether London could show a river like
the Seine—'Yes! We call it Fleet Ditch,' must have caused
some wonder as to the truth of his Lordship's reputed
politeness.

FLEET LANE was cut in two in the nineteenth century
by the formation of the London, Chatham and Dover

railway lines. In Stow's time the east end out of the Old Bailey to Seacoal Lane was called ST. GEORGE'S LANE. The name is preserved in the George Public House at that end. In Noorthouck's 1772 map St. George's Lane is called Little Old Bailey.

At the end of Fleet Lane was a stone bridge, called the Middle Bridge, ascended by fourteen steps; the arch of which was sufficiently high to allow a boat loaded with merchandise to pass under. In 1670 an Act was passed to make navigable the Fleet River from Bridewell Dock to Holborn Bridge. The river was reopened for vessels in November, 1673.

The second bridge over the river was Fleet Lane Bridge, near the Prison, which stood exactly where now is the Memorial Hall in Farringdon Street.

The third bridge was Fleet Bridge, connecting Fleet Street with Ludgate Hill, and stood about where now Ludgate Circus is. Ludgate Hill then terminated at St. Martin's, Ludgate. Thence to St. Paul's was Ludgate Street, formerly called Bowyer's Row.

Fleet Bridge, rebuilt in 1672, was taken down on 14 October 1765. Fleet Ditch was arched over, and the Fleet Lane Bridge vanished in the improvements when the Woolchurch or Stocks Market moved from the site of the present Mansion House to the newly named Fleet Market, commenced in September 1737 in the centre of Farringdon Street, where it remained until September 1829.

WARWICK LANE, Newgate Street, takes its name from an ancient house built there by an Earl of Warwick, Richard Nevill; who, in the thirty-sixth of Henry VI, the greater estates of the realm being called up to London, arrived with six hundred men all in jackets embroidered with ragged staves before and behind, and was lodged in Warwicke Lane; and in whose house there were oftentimes six oxen eaten at breakfast. Every tavern was full of the meat, for he that had any acquaintance in that house might have there so much of sodden and roast meat as he could prick and carry away upon a long dagger.

A stone bas-relief of Guy, Earl of Warwick, dated 1668, restored 1817, J. Deykes, Archt. and the letters G.C. (Guido comes, probably), still adorns a wall on the corner of the lane and Newgate Street.

The old name for this lane was ELDENESE LANE, or OLD DEAN'S LANE. Wren built the College of Physicians here, when their house at Amen Corner had been destroyed in the Great Fire, on part of the mansion of the old Earls of Warwick. Cutlers' Hall is now at No. 4. In a Harleian M.S. of 1555 this lane is called ALDEN'S LANE.

At the old Bell Inn in the lane Archbishop Leighton died in 1684. The Oxford Arms Inn, then on the west side, was the headquarters in London of the Oxford carrier, Edward Bartlett, who advertised that he also kept a hearse to convey a corpse to any part of England. He started his wagons and coaches three times every week. This was a fine old galleried inn with exterior staircases leading to the bedrooms. Dodsley mentions this lane as being OXFORD ARMS INN LANE.

CHAPTER III

FOLLOWING THE LINE OF OLD SEACOAL LANE ACROSS Holborn Viaduct is Snow Hill, the first lane on the right in which is COCK LANE, the scene of that famous ghost. This lane was, in the Middle Ages, the quarter to which common courtesans were publicly conducted and there made to abide, it having been ordered by Royal proclamation, *temp*. Edward I, that no such women should thenceforth reside within the walls of the City under pain of forty days' imprisonment. A list, too, was made of all such women, and a certain walk assigned to them. Civic ordinances were still more stringent against them at a later date; brothel-keepers, courtesans, and procuresses were to be driven by the Aldermen from their Wards, and, if found, to be forthwith taken by the Bedel and constables to one of the Sheriffs' Counters. No woman of ill fame was allowed to wear the fur called 'miniver' or the texture known as 'cendale' upon her hood or dress. From the Letter-Books we gather that in the middle of the fourteenth century most of these women were Flemish by birth.

Stow does not venture upon the derivation of the name of this lane. He would probably have liked to let it down lightly and suggest it was originally Cook Lane on account of the Pie corner—even as he suggested Stew Lane (the place of embarkment of incontinent women for the 'Stews')

63

was 'of a stew or hot house there kept'. The real reason seems, to me, to be rather more obvious.

I have mentioned this Cock Lane before in connection with Pie Corner and the figure of the fat boy upon a pedestal on the wall there. This was on a public-house called the 'Fortune of War' (a Field-Marshal's baton or a wooden leg), well known as a resort for body-snatchers and murderers who sold the bodies of their victims to the medical students at the Hospital.

The house of the 'ghost' was only demolished a few years ago. In 1876 it was occupied by a 'Gas' meter manufacturer (very appositely!) and was next door to a coal shop.

A girl of twelve was the impostor in the great ghost fraud. The daughter of a man named Parsons (the officiating clerk at St. Sepulchre's Church) was accustomed to sleep with a lady belonging to a family in Norfolk in her lodgings in the girl's father's house in the lane. This lady was said to have been poisoned by her husband with a doped glass of punch. The spirit of the departed lady was said to haunt the girl, who declared that an affirmative knock would be given that the dead woman would attend any of the eminent gentlemen, who wished to give their services for the detection of the crime, into the vault under the church of St. John, Clerkenwell, where her body lay. The Rev. Mr. Aldrich and Dr. Johnson, among many others, investigated the affair on the night of 1 February, 1762. Nothing was heard, and nothing happened. Dr. Johnson said the consensus of opinion was that the girl had some art of making a particular noise (she was said to scratch upon a board under her stays) and that there was no agency of any higher cause. The result was that Parsons, the girl's father,

Cock Lane, Snow Hill.

was put on the pillory three times and sentenced to imprisonment in the King's Bench prison for two years, Mrs. Parsons to one year, and Mary Frazer, who acted as interpreter of the noises, to six months with hard labour. Instead of pelting Parsons when in the pillory, the mob collected subscriptions for him!

The husband of the lady was said to have disobliged Parsons by leaving his lodgings and sueing him for some money he had lent him.

Garrick, in his *Prologue upon Prologues to the Deuce is in Him*, has:

> Yet still will you for jokes sit watching,
> Like Cock-lane ghost for Fanny's scratching.

Another Cock Lane was in Shoreditch, and is now called Boundary Street, probably because, as is stated on the north-west corner of the street, that is Shoreditch Borough Boundary.

Dr. Johnson, in his Life of Milton, tells us that Elizabeth, a daughter of Deborah, Milton's daughter, married a weaver in Spitalfields named Thos. Foster, and kept a chandler's shop in Cock Lane, near Shoreditch church. In 1750 *Comus* was played for her benefit. Wheatley says that this benefit, for which Dr. Johnson wrote a prologue, produced £130; but that Mrs. Foster (all of whose seven children had died) relapsed into indigence and the obscurity of her shop, and died in poverty in 1754. The first part of Church Street, here, was also part of Cock Lane, which had a right-angled form. NEW COCK LANE was a continuation of Cock Lane to Church Street, the next turning north to Bacon Street, Brick Lane.

The licensed house at the corner of Austin Street

F

and Cock Lane endeavours to bear out the farmyard meaning of the old name, being called the 'Conqueror'. My sketch shows it rebuilt, and one of the old weather-boarded and scallop-tiled houses in Austin Street, at the end of the lane, with the Church railings. In the church-yard are the old stocks and whipping-post.

Dodsley gives four Cock Lanes: One by Cock Hill (that was in Ratcliff Highway); a second near Falcon Lane, but does not say in which district (there are, or were, three Falcon Lanes); a third at Snowhill, and the fourth at Swan Fields, Shoreditch. An old COCK AND CASTLE LANE, at different times called CORK LANE and Castle Street, is now known as Crossways. It runs from Boleyn Road to the top end of Kingsland High Street on the opposite side to SHACKLEWELL LANE. The name is partly preserved in the Castle public-house.

Shacklewell Lane was the original entrance by road into the hamlet of Shacklewell. Part is now called Rectory Road, and goes due north till it reaches Stoke-Newington common, anciently known as Cockhanger-green.

Nearly parallel with Cock Lane, from King Street (old Cow Lane) into Smithfield runs HOSIER LANE, nearly all the houses in which at one time were of timber. Mr. J. T. Smith in his *Ancient Topography of London* depicts those which stood at the south corner, and says they were prob-ably of the time of James I. These were taken down in 1809. He tells us, too, that at the barber's shop at the corner, with the name Catchpole (good name for a barber —from two points of view!) over the door, was shown a short-bladed instrument said to be the identical dagger with which Walworth killed Wat Tyler.

Cock Lane, Shoreditch.

This lane is mentioned in a will, dated 1328, in which a shop there 'inhabited by Baroun' was demised to 'Emma, daughter of Adam de Drayton'.

Strype describes this lane as being 'of great resort during the time of St. Bartholomew's Fair, all the houses generally being made Publick for Tippling and Lewd sort of people'.

Once inhabited by Hosiers, Stow says that they 'are since removed into Cordwayner Street, the upper part thereof, by Bow Church, and last of all into Birchoveris Lane, by Cornehill' and that the 'Shoemakers and Curriers of Cordwayner Street removed, the one to St. Martin's-le-Grand, the other to London Wall near into Moorgate'.

Cordwayner Street was once called Hosier Lane and is now BOW LANE, at the north end of which stands Bow Church. The necessary proof of the claim to be an indisputable cockney is to have been born within sound of its bells.

For the maintenance of the great bell a worthy citizen, John Downe, left to the parish of St. Mary-le-bow two tenements in Hosier Lane. The ringing of the bell at 8 p.m. nightly was the signal for extinguishing lights in the Conqueror's time. In Edward II's reign the time was extended to 9 p.m. In 1469, by an order of Common Council, the bells were to be rung regularly at 9 p.m. and lights were to be exhibited in the steeple during the night to direct the traveller towards the metropolis. The bells and church were all burned in the Great Fire.

The church was first mentioned in William I's reign, and the present crypt dates from that period. The present church is built over and upon the arches of old Bow Church, erected in 1512 on the ruins of one built by the Conqueror

on the site of a Roman Temple, dedicated to the Virgin
and called 'le-Bow' from being built on arches or bows.
In 1769 Sir Christopher Wren finished the steeple, for the
erection and adornment of which, Dame Dyonis Wilkinson
gave £2,000. For the site of this steeple, two houses, between the church and Cheapside, were purchased. These
were probably the 'Crown Silde', a place for the Queen
and ladies of the court to view pageants and tournaments
in 'West Chepe'. It was originally a wooden building,
but it was pulled down and rebuilt by Edward III in
consequence of its falling when Queen Philippa and her
ladies were therein. In this year also the city paid £400
to the united parishes for the site of All Hallows Church
and Churchyard, on which to build the market in Honey
Lane. Part of this sum was appropriated to a set of bells.
Some fifty years later, much of the stone of the steeple had
become so decayed that it was decided to take down the
damaged part and rebuild it. When finished the dragon,
part of the support of the city arms, was announced to be
launched, regilt, and the City Cross printed red upon its
wings. Neale, one of the masons—with a flag—surmounted
the dragon, standing on a narrow bar, and the whole was
hauled up at one go to the block immediately over its
intended situation. As the clock struck one it was lowered
on to the polished steel spindle amid nine hearty cheers
from the committee, workmen and the immense number of
people in Cheapside, on St. Paul's galleries, the top of the
Monument and various other points of vantage, whence
they could see the dragon fly up with its rider. In the
dragon's mouth were a part of a glass of wine and some coins.
The dragon was of copper and was 8 feet 10 inches in length.

Bow Lane. E.C.

One of Mother Shipton's prophecies was that when the dragon of Bow Church and the grasshopper of The Royal Exchange should meet, London streets would be deluged with blood. In 1820 they were lying together in a stone-mason's yard, in Old Street Road, where—Timbs wrote—'the upper part of Wren's spire is preserved to this day'. As a matter of fact it wasn't Wren's spire. Though he was connected with the project of the rebuilding of the Exchange after the Great Fire, it was Edward Jerman, one of the City Surveyors, who rebuilt it under the direction of the Grand Joint Committee appointed for the purpose.

In 1284 the old Bow Church was placed under an inter-dict—closed for a week and all the windows stuffed with brambles in consequence of the hanging in the church of a man named Duckett. He had sought sanctuary there from having badly wounded a neighbour, whose friends found him in the night in the church and hanged him in a window. In the will of John Dunstaple, a skinner, 1307, he left property 'in a lane called "Le Bowe" in the parish of St. Michael de Paternoster's church'.

Parsons, the comedian, who died in 1795, was the son of a builder in Bow Lane. Another eminent inhabitant was Tom Coryat, the traveller who died in 1617. My sketch of Bow Lane shows the oldest house in it, at the corner of Watling Street, the Old Watling Restaurant, part of which is said to have withstood the Great Fire.

GOOSE LANE, in Bow Lane, is mentioned by Stow as being by Bow Church. William Essex, mercer, had tene-ments there in Edward III's reign. Strype, in 1720, Dod-sley, in 1761, call it Goose Alley. In Maitland's full list,

1739, the only Goose Lane, or Alley, is that by Fleet Ditch. In wills of 1336 and 1355 it is spelt GOSELANE. There is a GOOSELEY LANE off VICARAGE LANE, East Ham.

Bow Lane was another name for THIEVING or THEVEN LANE, Westminster, on account of its turning passage into old Broken Cross or Long Ditch. Strype said the houses were not over well built, and divers of its tenants drive a trade in second-hand goods.

The site is nearly represented by Great George Street. Stow explains—'Westminster, at the very entrance to the Close thereof is a lane that leadeth toward the West, called Thieving Lane, for the Thieves were led that way to the Gate House, while the Sanctuary continued in force.'

A THEVEN LANE is mentioned in a sixteenth-century document in the Bodleian Library, on the topography and divisions of the ancient parish of Stepney. 'The Ward of Mylend beginneth at Murkwalm Gate, at the West ende of Theven Lane so goynge be The Old Bussh with the part of Bromfeld into Belbarboureslane into Ffers Heth', etc. In this same document a reference is made to another lane. The wording runs:

The warde of Algat Strete begynneth at the myddil wale of Wastl . . . unto the Abbote's Mill of Tourehile soo goyng over a parte of . . . thes felds unto TREWMAN's LANE & unto Saynte Mary Spet[al] soo unto Smelockis Welle & so forth unto Murkwal & to Saynte [Thomas] Oke & ther departeth Myleinde & Algat Strete.

'THEEVES LANE by St. Thomas' Hospital', says Stow. It was probably wiped out by London Bridge Station and the railway—I cannot trace it.

Returning to Bow Lanes, there is now one of that name

running from 174 East India Dock Road to 223 Poplar High Street.

Past this Bow Lane at the east end of Poplar High Street is ROBINHOOD LANE.

West of this in Rocque's 1763 map was POPLAR LANE. This was either wiped clean out by the North London Railway or has been straightened out into the present Upper Crisp and Crisp Streets.

In Lockie's topography and map of 1816 is GUT LANE between Limehouse and Blackwall Reaches and the Isle of Dogs, running together with HARROW (marked ARROW in Rocque's 1763 map) LANE, nearly north and south. Harrow Lane is at 210 Poplar High Street now. Lockie, in mentioning Gut Lane, says 'See Dolphin Lane'. Probably it was called both. Near Gut Lane's south end is marked a 'Drunken Dock'. DOLPHIN LANE is at the entrance to Poplar Workhouse and DINGLE LANE (also spelt DANGLE) by the L.C.C. Schools further along. ANGEL LANE was destroyed in the formation of the West India Docks. An Angel Lane is at Stratford, E.15, and another is marked in Rocque's 1763 map as running from TEMPLE MILLS LANE to the 'Green Man', now part of Leyton Road. BLIND LANE was the next lane to it, forming a junction with White Horse Lane off Barking Road. The same map gives another Blind Lane at Fortune Green. A third Blind Lane is at Chapel End.

Bow COMMON LANE runs from Upper North Street to Canal Road, Poplar. From 78 Bow Common Lane to High Street, Bromley, runs old DEVON'S LANE, now Road. In this lane nearly a century ago a widow lived in an old cottage on the site of the present No. 75. She had a son at sea. Expecting him back one Easter, she placed a Hot Cross Bun in the window. He did not arrive, nor did she ever hear more of him. But every Good Friday she put by a bun for him. When she died some kindly person collected all these buns, strung them together and suspended them from a beam.

The cottage became known as The Bun House. The bun was added annually, and the place became a refreshment house. A public-house was built on the site, and called 'The Widow's Son'. In the lease is a clause compelling the licensee to maintain the annual observance.

In Devon's Lane, the first on the left past Bruce Road from Bow Road was STARCH LANE, now Grace Street.

CHAPTER IV

DRURY LANE COULD ALMOST FILL A CHAPTER WITH ITS history, and tales. Called after the Drury family, who built a house in the lane, previously known as Via de Aldwych, it has seen royalty, romance, revelry and riots.

The Queen of Bohemia lived in Craven House, built on the site of part of Drury House, and with her royalty and romance went hand in hand, for she is said to have been privately married to the Earl of Craven, who rebuilt part of Drury House for her reception and accommodation.

Nell Gwynne was born in Coal Yard (now Goldsmith Street) at the Holborn end of the lane.

Nan Clarges, the Drury Lane blacksmith's daughter, became Duchess of Albemarle. Her mother was one of the notorious 'Five women barbers of Drury Lane', the account of whose exploits, as related by Killigrew, sent Charles II into fits of laughter.

I have heard this account was to be found in Grainger's *History of England*, but, alas! it is not. Was it ever written down?

For revelry, the 'White Lion' and the 'Crown Coffee House'—both then in the lane—probably divided the honours. The former was a great resort, at night, of the upper classes, for drinking and other amusements. The latter added to these attractions the 'Flash Cove's Parliament'

at the meetings of which each member of the Bar, tradesman, or man about town (everyone was welcome) took the
title of one of the Upper House.

Riots took place not seldom. In the seventeenth century
the mob pulled the Cockpit Theatre—then in an alley
called after its name, between Drury Lane and Wild Street
—to bits, and tore all the actors' wardrobes to shreds.

Dr. Donne, one-time Dean of St. Paul's, lived at Drury
House, in his earlier days. He and his wife enjoyed here the
hospitality of Sir Robert Drury for a considerable time.

The Earl of Aylesbury had a house here in 1667. Carlyle
says that Oliver Cromwell was living there in 1646. Lady
Alington's residence was also there. The Marquis of Argyll
lived there from 1634 to 1637.

Mrs. Bracegirdle, Madame Vestris, Sir Arthur Chichester,
and Hayman the artist were all inhabitants of this lane.

The woman from whom the principal character in
Middleton's play 'The Roaring Girl'—Moll Cutpurse—
was taken, had her habitat in the purlieus of Drury Lane.
Her real name was Mary Frith. She was said to have been
the first Englishwoman to smoke a pipe in the streets of
London. This woman was instrumental in bringing to
justice the Five Women Barbers.

> Did you ever hear the like,
> Did you ever see the game
> Of the five women barbers
> Who lived in Drury Lane?

is all I have been able to discover in Grainger's *History*.

The lower part of Drury Lane was once called Prince's
Street—in James I's time. 'Prince's' or vulgarly 'Printers',
Court brought that to memory.

Drury Lane Corner.

LEWKNOR'S LANE—now Charles Street—off Drury Lane, harboured the infamous Jonathan Wild, who kept a house of ill fame there, assisted by Jane Sprackley.

On the 2nd June, 18th of James I, Sir L. Lewkenor (after whom this lane was named) had before him, and bound over in recognizances of £40 apiece, four yeomen, Wm. Masters, James Chillister, Ralph Greene and Mark Mackshen, to answer for making an affray and drawing their swords in Drury Lane.

Much of the inhabited site of Lewknor's Lane was taken up by the White Horse Inn yard; the site had changed its name from Aldwych Close to White Hart Close. In the time of James I the lane was for long a rendezvous and nursery for loose women.

Drury Lane has had a chequered career. From being a fashionable quarter it became the opposite.

Sir Walter Besant in his *Survey* mentions as the effects of the Civil War upon Long Acre and Drury Lane in 1642 that everyone was broke and

as a finishing stroke it is added that the ladies who formed the greater part of the population of Covent Garden, Drury Lane and Long Acre were reduced to a condition which is described in a tract of the times as a 'lump of amazement'. For this quarter and these ladies existed not by its citizens, though the morals of the city were by no means without reproach, but by the visitors who in quiet times flocked to London.

Another description of the lane:

There is near Covent Garden a street known by the name of Drury, which before the days of Christianity was purchased by the Queen of Paphos, and is the only part of Great Britain where the tenure of vassalage is still in being.

All that long course of buildings is under particular districts, or ladyships, after the manner of lordships in other parts, over which matrons of known abilities preside and have, for the support of their age and infirmities, certain taxes paid out of the rewards of the amorous labours of the young. This seraglio of Great Britain is disposed into convenient alleys and apartments, and every house from the cellar to the garret is inhabited by nymphs of different orders, that persons of every rank may be accommodated.

Thus Steele in the *Tatler*, 26 July 1709.

Pope, when he was twenty, wrote to Cromwell, 18 March 1708: 'In the town it is ten to one but a young fellow may find his strayed heart again with some Wild Street or Drury Lane damsel.'

Turnstile Alley in Drury Lane, opposite Great Queen Street, had such a 'wicket [*sic*] lot of people for inhabitants that it gained the name of "Dog and Bitch Yard"'.

The purlieus of Drury Lane were familiarly known as 'The hundreds of Drury'.

Goldsmith had his little say in the matter:

> Where the Red Lion, staring o'er the way,
> Invites each passing stranger that can pay.
> Where Calvert's Butt and Parson's black champagne
> Regale the drabs and bloods of Drury Lane.

NEWTONER'S LANE (now Newton Street), which runs by the west side of the Holborn Restaurant to PARKER'S LANE (now Street), was of so bad a reputation at the time of the Revolution that it was known as Little Sodom.

Parker's Lane School was founded in the lane of that name about 1663, by William Skelton of the parish of St. Giles-in-the-Fields, for the education of fifty poor boys; thirty-five of whom were to be of the parish of St. Giles,

Drury Lane, looking north.

ten of St. Martin's-in-the-Fields, and five of St. Paul's Cathedral. The Master had a salary of £20; two chaldrons of coal and a gown every year for teaching reading, writing and arithmetic (the three R's); each child to have a coat of six shillings price, every year; the surplus arising from the estate to be employed in putting the children out as apprentices.

At the east corner of Drury Lane and Maypole Alley was the forge of John Clarges, the blacksmith, father of Nan, who afterwards became Duchess of Albemarle. At this time, MAGPYE LANE was the old name for Newcastle Street, to which name it was changed in 1711, in honour of John Holles, Duke of Newcastle, then the ground landlord.

MAYPOLE LANE is mentioned in an Act for the Preventing of the Multiplicity of Buildings in and about the Suburbs of London, 1656, speaking of ground in Stanhope Street, along a dead wall from the end of Blackmoor Street to Maypole Lane in St. Clement's Parish.

LITTLE DRURY LANE was also called Maypole Alley at one time; long after the maypole had vanished.

Two tradesmen's tokens exist, Nos. 413 and 414 in the Guildhall, one: Anthony Hall in—Two crossed daggers, in the field. Reverse: Little Drury Lane—in the field. The other is curious: Richard Rich in litel—A wheatsheaf (A. W. H.); bird on top. Reverse: Drury Lane. Changer —of Farthinge. Was the latter man an agent in the collecting and interchanging with the issuers of farthing tokens? One other instance occurs: No. 690. At the White Beare—Bear with collar, and H.E.M. Reverse: In Kent Street—A Farthing changer.

Somewhere in the neighbourhood of Drury Lane was a

PHŒNIX LANE. This was referred to as being the lane in which, in the third year of James II, Mary Aubrey, a French nurse, had murdered her husband, Denis Aubrey, who had grossly ill-treated her, on one occasion having bitten her like a dog, and threatened to murder her. Fearing for her life she, when he was asleep, strangled him with her garter, in a quarter of an hour. Next morning the half-distraught woman went to the house where her son, by a former marriage, was working and asked his master for the loan of him—as he could speak English and French —to act as interpreter to a caller. When they reached home she showed him the lifeless body. Together they cut it up. She placed the trunk in her petticoat, carried her burden through Castle Street into Drury Lane, and thence to Parker's Lane, where she left it. She left the limbs in the Savoy, and threw the head into the outhouse of a friend. Some of the remains being discovered she was suspected and was taken at midnight, by a constable, a Monsieur Tard, a friend of her husband, who complained of him being missing, and a man named Richards, a tavern-keeper, from the house at which she was stopping in Phœnix Lane. This I think to have been a later name for Pitt Place, then the third turning on the left in Drury Lane, southwards from Long Acre. This was where the old Cockpit Theatre was situate, pulled down by the mob in 1617 and the Phœnix Theatre built on its site. This theatre gave way to Drury Lane Theatre. I cannot trace any Phœnix Lane anywhere near Drury Lane, unless it be the present Phœnix Street, off Dyott Street, which is quite likely. This is next to Church Lane, of which there are— or were—about fourteen in and around London. The one

Drury Lane. looking South.

—now called Allhallows Lane—in Thames Street has already been mentioned; as has Church Lane (now Street) Kensington.

Others of the same name are, or were, at Islington at 57 Essex Road; at Whitechapel—71 High Street. That is a short turning by the side of Whitechapel Parish Church to 27 Commercial Road East. Spectacle Alley runs into and forms a delta of shops with Whitechapel Road. It at one time extended to Cable Street. That part from Commercial Road to Cable Street is now called BACK CHURCH LANE. St. Giles-in-the-Fields; Tower Street; 456 Strand; Hampstead; Rag Fair; White Street, Southwark; Chelsea; Old Street; Hammersmith, and Fore Street, Limehouse, are the remainder, making fourteen in all.

Church Lane, St. Giles-in-the-Fields, is out of Dyott Street, and was renamed Bucknall Street, in 1878. In the Post Office List for 1857 it is given as Church Lane, George Street, St. Giles; that being after Dyott Street (in consequence of a murder being committed there) had been renamed. It is once more Dyott Street.

Stow says there were two Church Lanes out of Great Tower Street, both so called because 'one runneth down by the East side of St. Dunstan's Church and the other by the West end of same. Out of the West lane turneth another lane West toward St. Marie Hill and is called Fowle Lane, which is for the most part in Tower Street Ward.' That would be the present Cross Lane.

Church Lane, Strand, was at No. 456, thirty doors on the left from Charing Cross, in 1816.

Church Lane, Hampstead, runs from High Street to Heath Street.

The one in Rag Fair (or ROSEMARY LANE), Wellclose Square, which ran to Whitechapel High Street, is now split into two names: Church Lane from the High Street to Commercial Road; from there to Caber Street it is Back Church Lane. A few turnings east of this in Commercial Road—at No. 138—was UMBERSTONE LANE, now Road.

By the side of St. George's Church, Borough, was a Church Lane (afterwards Street) which is now incorporated with its continuation White Street in Long Lane there.

The Chelsea Church Lane is an ancient thoroughfare, built upon at an early period, but principally since the rectory was removed hither, in 1569, from Millman's Row.

In this lane lived Thomas Shadwell, Poet Laureate.

Dr. Atterbury went there in the 1690's. Dean Swift in 1711 came to live opposite him. In his journal to Stella:

I go there with Patrick and my portmanteau, for sixpence, and pay six shillings a week for one silly room, with confounded coarse sheets. I lodge just over against Dr. Atterbury's house; and yet, perhaps, I shall not like the place better for that.

A famous old inn, the 'White Horse' in this lane, was unfortunately burned down. A new one was built. The old one contained some fine ancient panelling, grotesque escarpments and carvings, especially of human figures in the form of brackets. Mr. Thomas Faulkner says he was present at a stag hunt, in 1796, when the stag turned up Church Lane, and took refuge in Mrs. Hutchins' barn there—where he was taken alive.

There is a Church Lane at Tooting from the Common to Mitcham Road; another at Charlton, from the village to Woolwich Road; one was at Stoke Newington—the first turning on the right past West Hackney Church; yet one more off Old Street. In fact there is a Church Lane in nearly every outlying district of London—Battersea, Ealing, East Finchley, Hornsey, Kingsbury, Leytonstone, Lower Edmonton, Merton, Tottenham, Walthamstow, Willesden, Hammersmith, etc. There was a Church Lane off ELEPHANT LANE, which latter is off Rotherhithe Street, Bermondsey.

A Church Lane, formerly called VANNER'S LANE, after Henry Vanner who owned it in 1354, ran south out of Upper Thames Street to the river at Three Cranes' Wharf, opposite the church of St. Martin Vintry. This lane was absorbed into the footway of Queen Street since the widening thereof. Before the widening in 1846–7 the southern portion of Queen Street was called BROAD LANE. Stow says it was called BRODE LANE as being 'broder for the passing of carts from the Vintry warfe than be the other lanes'. In 1335 Henry de Bydyk bequeathed for life certain rents in 'the lane called LE BRODELANE in the parish of St. Martin de Bermanscherche' (this was St. Martin-in-the-Vintry).

CHURCHAW LANE, previously called STEPHEN'S LANE (in the parish of St. Magnus de Briggestrete justa Oystergate 17 Edward III), and then Churchyard Alley at 119 Upper Thames Street, west of Old London Bridge (according to Elme's *Topography*, 1831), was removed about that year for part of the approaches to the new London Bridge. The site is now occupied by Adelaide Place. STEPHENES-

LANE is mentioned in a will of Henry Lambyn dated 1329.

CHURCH ROAD LANE (now Church Row) in Commercial Road East, opposite SALMON'S LANE, was once part of ROSE LANE. This Rose Lane is by Stepney Station, from London Street to Horseferry Road. In Rocque's map of 1763 it is quite a long lane, running from White Horse Lane, turning south opposite the end of Salmon's Lane and continuing down the west side of Limehouse Church, which part has been just referred to as having been called Church Road Lane, now Church Row. OAK LANE is out of Church Row, westwards to Northey Street.

In Large's *Way about London* is given another Rose Lane as being along Commercial Road East to the fourth turning on the right past Stepney railway station, which is Island Row, then down Island Row to the first turning on the right. In Fashion Street, Spitalfields, was another Rose Lane, now, I think, called Brick Lane. A ROSE AND CROWN LANE runs out of GREAT CHURCH LANE, Fulham Palace Road, Hammersmith. CHURCHYARD LANE is in St. Thomas Street, Southwark.

While dealing with the neighbourhood of Chelsea—the southern end of the present Flood Street was once known as ROBINSON'S LANE. The upper end was called Queen Street. Then the whole length was named Queen Street, afterwards Flood Street. The first turning on the right there is now Robinson Street. Another Robinson's Lane was at Poplar.

Coming towards Pimlico from Chelsea is TURPENTINE LANE—so called, I should think, in connection with a white-lead manufactory which, at one time, stood at the lower end. This is a curious lane—a long massive granite-setted passage, with a cart-wheel track, running from Ebury Bridge, between the back of Westmorland Street (it was there long before this street was built, as shown in the 1772 map) and the buildings called the 'Avenue' of the Peabody Trust Pimlico Estate.

It is almost a cutting at the lower end, where it makes a serpentine bend and comes out at 120 Grosvenor Road.

Near here was old BAKER'S LANE, now called Sutherland Street. Then Warwick Street was known as Willow Walk, and that part of Lupus Street from Baker's Lane to Ranelagh Road was Cross Lane.

Among the western lanes were BROMPTON LANE (the western end of the present Brompton Road), off which ran GORE LANE, up to Kensington Gore. CROMWELL LANE —now Road—was the next lane westwards.

BROOKFIELD LANE, now all Kensington Place at 149 Church Lane (now Street), Notting Hill Gate end, at one time was so called only as far as Johnson's Place.

Another Brookfield Lane is at Wick Road, Hackney.

CHAPTER V

Lﾞondon Lane is at Hackney and runs from 223 Mare Street to 18 Tower Street, and is one of the most unpicturesque places imaginable. In view of its name and the title of this book I have inflicted upon the public a drawing of it. The garden of a well-built mansion once in this lane was thrown in with that of a large house then in Mare Street, just opposite the Catholic Apostolic Church, and each house formed either the male or female departments of a lunatic asylum, the proprietors of which were Doctor Oxley and Doctor Ayre, his son-in-law. The former might be accounted one of the fathers of teetotalism. Even when compelled to use a bath chair, he was to be seen distributing tracts dealing with this hobby. His creed did not influence the treatment of his patients—according to accounts rendered to many of the friends of patients under his care. Part of this lane is called Nelson Terrace. At No. 23 is a turning with the name of Gransden Avenue —a private road shut in by four posts and a hinged bar gate. I see Gransden's piano works there. Anything less like a lane than this! But it is a present-day London Lane and is actually so named. So here it is—as it is! London Fields Railway Station is just here and the railway bridge over the lane adds nothing to the picturesque amenities of it. I stood under it to make my sketch upon the same

London Lane

principle as the reason given by the Parisian who informed a friend that he had taken a flat in the Eiffel Tower. 'What on earth for?' asked the friend. 'Because it's the only place from which I can't see the —— thing.'

POND LANE, in Hackney, was the old name for Lea Bridge Road (before 1750 when a bridge for carriages over the river was constructed), now Mill Fields Road. In Rocque's and earlier maps Church Street commenced at London Lane, the dividing line between South Hackney and the northern parish of St. John-at-Hackney. More recently MORNING LANE was accounted so.

HACKNEY LANE was the old name, over two hundred years ago, of the High Road, Clapton, main road from the corner where Urswick Road, formerly Upper Homerton, ends. In Rocque's map of 1745 Hackney Lane embraced High Road, Upper Clapton, from Northfield Road to Stamford Hill Gate.

BOB'S HALL LANE was that part of the main road to Clapton where Clapton Square—once Clapton Fields—is.

BACK LANE was the old name of Clarence Road (a back road to Clapton coming out where Clapton Road still does at the Pond), now a thriving thoroughfare.

I have traced twelve Back Lanes. Back Lane, Kennington, ran from Penton Place to New Street. Salisbury and De Laune Streets, at the back of Kennington Theatre in Kennington Park Road, occupy the site of the lane. Back Lane, Evelyn Street, Deptford, is now Czar Street. It was once called BUTT LANE, with a toll-gate at the end of it, at entrance to Flaggon Row, according to 'Ambulator' in 1798, in the *Gentleman's Magazine*.

Back Lane, described in an old book of cab fares dated

1801, is given as being 31 poles in length, and as running from Paradise Street, Rotherhithe, to Church Street. It has disappeared.

Back Lane, East Smithfield, is now swallowed up by Cable Street. In 1806, about 2 a.m. one day, a stack of chimneys in the centre of two very old houses fell in, carrying with it the houses themselves down to the ground floor. Fifteen people were badly injured, and two killed. In the 1829 map VINEGAR LANE is marked as running between Commercial Road and old Back Lane (now Cable Street). It was opposite Jamaica Street at the north end. The present Hardinge Street is evidently on the site of the old lane. Another Vinegar Lane was by the old Vinegar Works between Meadow Road and South Lambeth Road, at the back of Fentiman Road.

High Street, Lambeth, was called Back Lane, says Allen, in 1828. There was a Back Lane at Old Brompton.

According to Dodsley there was a lane of this name off Three Hammer Alley, Tooley Street, and another one from Clerkenwell Road (then Liquor Pond Street) to Ray Street. This is now called Back Hill. The same authority quotes another as being near Sun Tavern Fields, Shadwell. The eleventh is marked in the 1918 P.O. Directory map, from Gervase Street to Asylum Road, Old Kent Road. The twelfth Back Lane is at Barking. As it is the only one of the name which still looks like one I have sketched it.

VAUXHALL LANE led from Vauxhall Stairs to the old Vauxhall Gardens.

WORKHOUSE LANE was a continuation of Broad Street from the Albert Embankment, and now part of a wide Prince's Road.

Back Lane, Barking.

WHITEPOST LANE is the parish boundary between Hackney and Old Ford. There is another WHITE POST LANE at 917 Old Kent Road, and according to *Names of Streets, etc., for* 1920, also one at Peckham. From Manor Park to East Ham ran yet another White Post Lane.

Morning Lane—Dodsley, in 1761, spells it MOURNING—is at 300 Mare Street, Hackney. In Rocque's map, 1745, it is called MONEY LANE. A shop at the corner (which used to be a grocer's) was—nearly three centuries ago—a famous public-house called the 'Green Man', which, according to a brass token in the British Museum, was kept by John Braine, in 1667. This bears the figure of a man with a club in his right hand, and on reverse 'In Hackney, 1667, his halfpenny'. Morning Lane was once the central road of communication with the hamlet of Homerton.

Off this lane at No. 40 runs Fox's LANE. FOX LANE was the old name of the southern end of the present Mayfield Road, the first on the right down Middleton Road from Kingsland Road.

Another Fox Lane is at Upper Shadwell.

LAMB LANE is at 177 Mare Street, Hackney. At the corner was an old residence, built about 1720, with trees and a small court. Then an older house, standing further back with a large and productive kitchen garden, occupied for years by a wealthy goldsmith, was supposed to have been the residence of Sir Walter Raleigh. A fine old mulberry tree was in this garden. Small cottages are now erected here, built in 1832, according to a plaque upon the wall which also informs us that 'The property of H. D. Hacon Esqre. extends to 6 ft. south of this stone'. Again the railway bridge across the lane detracts from

the amenities. 'The Old Lamb' public-house—now but
an off-licence—from which the lane took its name, is not
now even included in the numbers, being designated No. 1
Sidmouth Street, upon the corner of which it stands.
Higher up the lane are St. Michael's Schools and Hall, all
built of stone, and dated 1874. The Church of St. Michael
and All Angels is at the top corner facing London Fields.
The Vicarage on the right is a fine stone building and the
L.C.C. Schools are of stone to match.

It is a natural progression from a lamb to a sheep.
SHEEP LANE runs from Westgate Street to Andrew's Road;
Westgate Street being at 117 Mare Street. It runs from
London Fields East to the canal and gasworks, and con-
tains some rather squalid cottages. On the right is Urban
Place, in which, anyhow, there are six trees, though the
front gardens are but apologies for such.

The odour of the lane is pleasingly tempered by that
emitted from Messrs. Potter & Moore's scent factory of
Lavender from Mitcham just adjacent in Ash Grove.

This Sheep Lane is marked MUTTON LANE in Rocque's
map of Hackney dated 1745.

Mutton Lane, as marked on 1840 map, runs from Mare
Street across Sheep Lane at London Fields East. A small
brook or watercourse, long since vanished, ran through
the heights of Highgate and through Canonbury, crossed
Kingsland Road, having over it a small stone bridge.
Thence skirting the west side of London Fields, it flowed
towards the 'Cat and Mutton'. This brook was dispersed
by excavations for the Regent's Canal, for a few years
leaving a small dry ditch crossed by a bridge just where
the Broadway passes into Goldsmith's Row.

Vine S.^t old Hatton Garden Clerkenwell
from Ford Lane London W.C.

In this same 1840 map a Mutton Lane is given opposite RED COW LANE in Mile-End Road, running into the Dog Row (now Cambridge Road). This Mutton Lane is now called Assembly Passage.

Red Cow Lane was by the Turnpike in Mile-End Road. It is now Cleveland Street.

About half a mile below the old Turnpike is White Horse Lane, the upper part of which was marked George Street in map of 1829. This same map shows this lane as running into the Cow Lane now Ben Jonson Road.

The old GLOBE LANE at 191 Mile-End Road is now Globe Road. It was given in Cary's old cab-fare list, 1801, as being 1 furlong 14 poles from Stepney Green, between that and White Horse Lane (which is given as being 8 poles further eastward).

The first turning on the west side of Globe Lane or Road is curiously named XX Place.

Mutton Lane in Clerkenwell, so called from having been 'much frequented by courtesans' who were styled 'laced muttons', has disappeared. The present Vine Street, in which there are steps leading up to Rosebery Avenue, marks part of the site of old Mutton Lane. My sketch shows that end of it.

When, in 1678, the Hampstead Ponds overflowed after a severe storm, the Fleet Channel grew into a torrent. Several thousands of pounds' worth of damage were done in Coldbath Fields, Mutton Lane, Peter Street and the vicinity.

A SHEEPCOTE LANE is to be found between Henley Street and Latchmere Road, Battersea Park. There was a SHEPHERDS LANE at Homerton.

In 1816 there was a BEAST LANE at Stepney which ran from the west end of the church towards Whitechapel. Lockie says 'refer to BULL LANE'. But in the 1857 map Bull Lane runs from Whitehorse Street on the north side of the church to High Street, Stepney. This is incorporated in the present Ben Jonson Road. So that Beast, Bull, and Cow lanes may have been, if not the same, at least very near neighbours. Ben Jonson Road runs from the High Street to Rhodeswell Road.

Out of this Whitehorse Street to Commercial Road East runs SALMON'S LANE.

Whitehorse Street on the east, the two sides of Rhodeswell Road, on the north and west, and Salmon's Lane on the south form an irregular square enclosing many mean streets and part of Regent's Canal.

SERMON'S LANE, which at one time ran into Salmon's Lane, appears to have been part of the now Rhodeswell Road, evidently so called from old Rhodeswell Common, which was south-west of old Bow Common. Dodsley gives another Sermon Lane at Limehouse, but this is probably the same.

In the *List of Principal Streets, etc.*, issued by the P.O. in 1857 the now Mantell Street at 55 Liverpool Road, Islington, to White Conduit Street, is named Sermon Lane.

Sermon Lane in the City, from Carter Lane to Knightrider Street, was, says Stow,

corruptly called this for SHEREMONIER'S LANE, for I find it called by that name recorded in the fourteenth of Edward I, and in that Lane a place to be called the Blacke loft (of melting silver) with four shops adjoining.

Sermon Lane

It may therefore be well supposed that lane to take name of Sheremonyars, such as cut and rounded the plates to be coined or stamped into sterling pence; for the place of coining was the Old Exchange, near unto the said Sheremonier's Lane.

In Historical MSS. 1315, Sir Nicholas Housebonde, minor canon of St. Paul's, had assigned to him a house at the north-east corner of SERMOUNERERE's LANE. He complained that it was inconvenient for the purpose on account of the grievous perils which were to be feared by reason of its distance from the Cathedral and the crossings of dangerous roads by night, and the attack of robbers and other ill-disposed persons which he had already suffered, and also on account of the ruinous condition of the building and the crowd of loose women who lived round it. Castle Baynard Ward School was here, the quaint figures on which were preserved by Messrs. Cook, Son & Company, who took over the building for the extension of their premises.

My drawings of Sermon Lane and Carter's Lane were bought from me by Mr. Arthur Pragnell, lately a retired partner in Messrs. Cook, Son & Company. He has very kindly lent them to me for reproduction here. They show two of the many overhead passages connecting different departments in this big mercantile firm.

When giving the measurements of the longest lanes in London, I omitted all mention of MARYLEBONE LANE. As the present High Street, Marylebone, was all part of the lane before it was built upon in about 1680, it must all be included. According to Cary's measurement in 1801 the length of High Street was 2 furlongs 30 poles, and that of Marylebone Lane 3 furlongs 1 pole; the total length would be 5 furlongs 31 poles. This makes it the third longest, pride of place being given to Brick Lane and Park Lane.

As late as the commencement of the seventeenth century, Marylebone was a small village surrounded by fields and three-quarters of a mile distant from the Metropolis. Glover in 1820 sketched and painted Primrose Hill and neighbourhood from Clarence Gate. In his pictures are shown haymakers in the fields and only three buildings scattered about near where the present church stands. The old winding lane led to the old village of Tybourn, the church of which is supposed to have stood on the site of Marylebone Court House. Human bones have been unearthed there upon each occasion of its rebuilding. This points to the fact of there having been a churchyard there. In the fourteenth century Tybourn Church was in a deserted and lonely position. From its proximity to the road from London—now Oxford Street—marauders who infested the road made frequent visits to the church, which from being so often robbed became neglected and dilapidated, so that the inhabitants petitioned Braybrooke, the then Bishop of London, to allow them to remove it to a place where they had erected a chapel. A new church dedicated to St. Mary was then built. As this was near the Tybourn Brook it began to be distinguished by that addition and the village was called Mary-bone, now Mary-le-bone. Being in a ruinous condition about 1740 that church was taken down. The new church was taken by Hogarth for the scene of the Rake's marriage to a deformed and superannuated female.

Clement's Lane E.C.

In a map published in 1742 the small church is shown detached from London with two zigzag ways leading to it—one near Vere Street, then the western extreme of the new buildings, and the other from Tottenham Court Road. This zigzag way, then, as now, Marylebone Lane, near Vere Street, was the communication between the High Road and the village. Rows of houses with their backs to the fields extended from St. Giles' Pound to Oxford Market, on the site of which are now built Oxford and Cambridge Mansions. The fields about this lane were laid out in streets about 1767. In a map of 1720 a part of the brook is shown forming a little island near what is now Wigmore Street.

Henry III was responsible for first bringing into use for the citizens of London the waters of this brook 'for the profit of the city, and good of the whole realm, thither repairing; to wit for the poor to drink and the rich to dress their meat' and 'with liberty to convey water from Teyborne by pipes of lead into the City'.

The great conduit in West Cheape was the first—in 1236. In Lea & Glynne's map of 1700 one conduit head is shown to have behind the Banqueting House erected in what is now Stratford Place; at which, every year on the 18th September, a banquet was given on this gala day, to the Lord Mayor, Alderman and City authorities, to inspect the Conduit-heads.

Another head was at the corner of Marylebone Lane, pointed out by a stone let into a house close to Wigmore Street, dated 1776; one higher up at the bend of the lane and two on the south side of Oxford Street.

In 1747 Marylebone Lane and the brook bounded this

part of London. About twenty years later, the whole of the site of the conduits and Banqueting House was laid out in streets. The lane then ran, as has been mentioned, right up to Marylebone Park, which as late as Queen Elizabeth's time afforded excellent cover for game. In here, besides a ranger, was a keeper who received a salary of £12 13s. 4d., and a keeper of the woods and gardens who received £10.

Macaulay tells us that at the end of the reign of Charles II, cattle fed and sportsmen wandered with guns and dogs over the site of the borough of Marylebone. In the Board of Works accounts for 1582 is an entry of payment 'for making of two new standings in Marylebone and Hyde Park for the Queen's Majestie and the Noblemen of France to see the hunting'.

In the year 1600, on 3 February, ambassadors from the Emperor of Russia and their retinue rode through the City of London to Marylebone Park and 'there hunted at their pleasure'.

A piece of the old iron railing which enclosed this Park was to be seen at No. 8 Portland Place. Foley House had much of the railings and gates.

At the Middlesex Sessions, 12 February twenty-fifth of Elizabeth, three men were bound over to appear at the next General Sessions of the Peace 'for takinge of hinges from the gate of Marybone Parke'.

Dickens lived from 1840—when he removed from Doughty Street—till 1850 at the north-west corner of Marylebone Lane. This is known as No. 1 Devonshire Terrace. It will be seen in my sketch—a double bow-fronted house in the gardens enclosed by a high wall.

Marylebone Lane.

Here he kept a pet raven, which gave rise to an actual rumour that he had gone 'raven' mad! Longfellow stayed here with him. In a letter from him dated 16 October 1841 are the words: 'I write this from Dickens' study, the focus from which so many luminous things have radiated. The ravens croak in the garden, and the ceaseless roar of London fills my ears.' It is said that though now Marylebone Lane ends on the north side of Oxford Street, it formerly continued in a winding manner by Marylebone Street and SHUG LANE to the Haymarket.

Shug Lane was a continuation of Marylebone Street, and ran from Sherwood Street to Coventry Street at the top of the Haymarket. Denman Street was then Queen Street, and the southern end of Warwick Street, now demolished, was part of Marylebone Street. Old Tichborne Street was, I believe, a later name for part of Shug Lane.

Chatelain, the celebrated engraver, lodged at a carpenter's shop in Shug Lane, where he died in 1770 of indigestion after a hearty supper out of doors, of lobster, and a hundred head of asparagus eaten after his arrival home.

The north side of this lane was pulled down for the opening up of Regent Circus, Piccadilly, from the bottom corner of Great Windmill Street to the corner of Sherwood Street, and the formation of Shaftesbury Avenue. Woodstock Street would have been part of the said lane by its lie. Both South Molton Street and SOUTH MOLTON LANE would have been too far west.

In the *New View of London*, 1708, is certainly the explanation—Marylebone Street, built about 1680, led from

HEDGE LANE (now Whitcomb Street) to Marylebone; 'a pretty straight street between Glasshouse Street and Shug Lane, near Piccadilly'.

In one of the green fields between Marylebone and London, Lord Townsend and Lord Bellemont fought a duel in which the latter was dangerously wounded by a bullet through the groin.

The *Daily Journal* in 1728 states 'many persons arrived in London from their country houses in Marylebone'.

On the east side of Marylebone Lane, a little north of Manchester and Cavendish Squares, were Marylebone Gardens, a place of fashionable amusement founded towards the end of the seventeenth century, in the grounds of which was the tavern 'The Rose of Normandy'—then the oldest house in the parish. Built in the seventeenth century, it had

fruit trees, gravel walks 204 paces long, 7 broad; the circular wall 485 paces long, 6 broad; the centre square, a bowling green, 112 paces one way, 88 another—all, except the first, double set with quickset hedges, full grown, and kept in excellent order, and indented like town walls.

Here Sheffield, Duke of Buckingham, bowled time away in the days of Pope and Gay. The latter alludes to the place more than once in his *Beggar's Opera*.

This was the scene of 'The Upas in Marybone Lane' by James Smith, two verses of which I quote:

> Britannia this Upas-tree bought of Mynheer,
> Removed it through Holland and planted it here;
> 'Tis now a stock plant of the genus wolf's-bane,
> And one of them blossoms in Marybone Lane.'

The house that surrounds it stands first in the row,
Two doors at right angles, swing open below;
And the children of misery daily steal in,
And the poison they draw they denominate Gin.

In the 1772 map Hedge Lane (mentioned above) runs from Cockspur Street, or rather, Charing Cross—no Trafalgar Square then—to James Street; its continuation to Coventry Street being Whitcomb Street. In the 1840 map Pall Mall East and Trafalgar Square have been made and the lane is cut short at the former. It still, there, goes as far as James Street. In the meantime in an 1829 map Hedge Lane is plainly marked Dorset Place. It is now all called Whitcomb Street, from Pall Mall East to Coventry Street. Rocque in 1747 gives a Whitcomb's Court running out of Hedge Lane. The Duke of Monmouth lived in this lane before removing to Monmouth House, Soho Square.

In 1821 some interesting ruins were found at the bottom of the lane; part, it was thought, of the ruins of the Royal Mews burnt in 1534. In Aggas's plan of London, Hedge Lane is shown as a country lane actually bounded by hedges.

At the south-east corner near Charing Cross was HARTSHORN LANE, demolished in 1760 and Northumberland Street built in its stead. In MSS. of the time of James I this is called 'Hartshorne Lane or Christopher Alley'.

In Fuller's *Worthies* he states *re* Ben Jonson:

Though I cannot with all my industrious enquiry, find him (B.J.) in his cradle, I can fetch him from his long coats. When a little child he lived in Hartshorne Lane, near Charing Cross, where his mother married a bricklayer for her second husband.

H

Sir Edmund Berry Godfrey's Woodwharf was at the bottom of this lane.

Just east of this before coming to the Station is BREWER'S LANE, at No. 15 Strand, a quaint place of wine merchants' vaults and stores coming out near the bottom of Villiers Street. Lockie gives a Brewer's Lane as being in Greenwich Street, Thames Street; and called Grantham's Lane in Stow's time after John Grantham, Mayor in 1328–9, who had a house built of stone in the lane. Ralph Dodman, mayor (and a brewer), dwelt there in 1529. The house was afterwards turned into a brewhouse—hence the name. As a matter of fact, before it was known as Grantham's the lane was called BATHESTERE'S LANE, and in 1343 John Grantham blocked the way to the Thames with two large stones and two borders of iron, and called that end by his own name before it was used as a brewhouse and the whole lane called Brewers Lane at 83 Upper Thames Street.

There are four lanes actually called BREWHOUSE LANE. One runs from High Street, Wapping, to OLD GRAVEL LANE. In it are the City Soap Works, Messrs. D. & N. Gibbs, Limited, and the L.C.C. School. Lockie says this was called Brewhouse Lane on account of Pickard's Brewery. Old CINNAMON LANE, now Street, is opposite the end of this Brewhouse Lane, across Old Gravel Lane.

There was a Brewhouse Lane in Salisbury Court, Fleet Street. I am sorry to say I cannot verify this—I have mislaid the note with my information, and can only record the bare fact. Another one runs from Putney Bridge Road to Douglas Wharf and the fourth is a no-thoroughfare lane at Church Street, Greenwich.

I have mention of a BREWERY LANE at Nine Elms, but no data, except that it is given in the P.O. *List of Principal Streets and Places* for April, 1857—the date is not given as the first of that month.

And I hear of another in Old Kent Road, but have not been able to trace it.

Old Gravel Lane, above mentioned, opposite Green Wharves, High Street, Wapping, was so called from the carts loaded with gravel passing through it to the Thames, when the gravel was employed in ballasting ships, before ballasting was taken out of the river.

A terrible tragedy occurred on 19 December 1811 at the King's Arms then here. The landlord (Williamson), his wife and the female servant were murdered by Williams, a sailor. An apprentice lodging there escaped by tying sheets to the bedpost and letting himself down into the street.

NEW GRAVEL LANE (so called to distinguish it from the Old) was used for the same purpose. It runs from 22 Shadwell High Street to Wapping Wall.

Dodsley gives another New Gravel Lane as opposite Horselydown New Stairs. In Noorthouck's 1772 map this is marked NEW LANE. In a map of 1840 the same lane is shown there (but not named) running into Gainsford Street as before. This lane is called Maguire Street in later maps.

Of ordinary GRAVEL LANES there are three.

In the one at 148 Houndsditch, on the east side near Aldgate Church, was a fine old house called 'Ambassador's House', occupied at one time by the Spanish Ambassador. Stow called it a garden-house 'built amid fair hedge-rows of elm trees with bridges and easie stiles to pass over into the pleasant fields'. What a contrast is this lane now! That was in the time of James I. It was situated in a courtyard with a fine gateway upon a flight of steps and approached by Seven Step Alley. On the first floor was a superb fireplace of coloured marble and carved oak, and a ceiling upon which were the arms of the founder, Robert Shaw, and those of the Vintner's Company, of which he was Master. This house was taken down in 1844. A view of it is in No. 2 of *The Archæological Album*.

Another Gravel Lane is at Wapping, running from St. George Street—the respectable modern name for the old familiar Ratcliff Highway—to Wapping High Street, between Wapping and the East Basins of the London Docks. Here was, in 1642, one of the Long Parliament's bulwarks 'on ye hill at ye north end of Gravel Lane', close by the Thames. Near this Gravel Lane along Green Bank was MEETING HOUSE LANE, 1 furlong 9 poles in length. Meeting House Lane now extends from Chandler Street only to Watts Street. Thence to Green Bank it is now renamed Raymond Street. Another Meeting House Lane runs from High Street, Peckham, to Asylum Road. Woolwich also has one—from High Street to Rodney Street.

At 147 Houndsditch there is a BACK GRAVEL LANE.

The third Gravel Lane, at Southwark, extended from Great Suffolk Street to the Falcon Stairs, Bankside, in an 1840 map. In one of 1894 it stops at Southwark Street. Zoar Street, where Bunyan is said to have often preached, ran out of this lane at a part which is now called Sumner Street. The river end of the old Gravel Lane is now part

of an extended Holland Street, which runs as far as Love
Lane and Sumner Street to the east. The latter, as has
been said, forms part of old Maid Lane.

A GREEN LANE used to run from Holland Street to
BEAR LANE, of which latter it was a northern continuation.
This also appears to be now part of an angled, extended
Holland Street. The forming of Southwark Street has
disturbed the topographical amenities round here. For
instance, opposite the end of Castle Street at Southwark
Bridge Road a sort of Delta was formed by BOAR's HEAD
LANE, Dirty Lane and Counter Lane from Red Cross
Street to the Borough High Street.

Bear Lane serves to remind us of the Bear baitings
which took place at the Paris Garden situate on the Bankside, west of St. Saviour's Church. Stow explains:

Now to returne to the west bancke: there were two
Beare gardens, the old and the newe, places wherein were
kept beares, bulls, and other beasts, to be bayted, as also
mastives in several kennels, nourished to bayt them.
These beares and other beastes are there bayted in plots
of ground scaffolded about for beholders to stand safe.

So far as safety went—well! It did go! One afternoon,
on a Sunday, in 1582, a fatal accident occurred which
gave a great shock to these diversions. The scaffold at the
Paris Garden, crowded with spectators, gave way; the
loss of many lives and many fractured limbs being
the result.

Paris Garden, according to old maps, extended from the
west end of Bankside and the Liberty of the Clink towards
what is now the southern extremity of Blackfriars Bridge.
In the centre of this Liberty stood a cross, the narrow lane

from which leading to the river was called OLDE PARRIS LANE. The Parish of Christ Church was originally part of the district called the Liberty of Paris Garden; this was so called after Robert of Paris, who, in the reign of Richard II, built a mansion here on the marsh, near the river.

The Bear Garden here was from a very early date and the entertainments continued till late in the reign of William III, when this species of amusement was then removed to Hockley-in-the-Hole, 'as more convenient for the butchers and such like', then the chief patrons of this once royal amusement. The Tudors and Stuarts enjoyed the sport, and it was a common custom to introduce a new ambassador to the Bear Garden as soon as his first audience was over.

Among MSS. in the British Museum is a warrant of Lord Arlington's, dated 28 March 1676, for the payment of £10 to James Davies, Esq., master of His Majesty's Bears, Bulls and Dogs, for making ready 'the roomes at the Bear Garden and Bayteing the Beares before the Spanish Ambassador, the 7th January last, 1675'.

Sunday was the day of exhibition during the reigns of Henry VIII and Elizabeth. To the disgust of Henslowe and Allen—who represented their losses to be very great in consequence—James I prohibited performances on that day. The sports were frequently very cruel. A pony was baited by dogs with a monkey on his back. One 'sport' was tying a bear to a stake and whipping him till the blood ran down his shoulders. Some of the bears were very famous. Harry Hunks is often referred to by Elizabethan writers, and the name of Sackerson is known to readers of *The Merry Wives of Windsor*.

Publias, student at the common law,
Oft leaves his books, and for his recreation,
To Paris Garden doth himself withdraw,
Where he is ravisht with such delectation,
As down among the bears and dogs he goes.
Where, whilst he skipping cries 'To Head! To Head!'
His satin doublet and his velvet hose
Are all with spittle from above be-spread:
Then is he like his father's country hall,
Stinking of dogges and muted all with hawks.
And rightly too on him this filth doth fall
Which for such filthy sports his books forsakes,
Leaving old Plowden, Dyer, and Brooke alone,
To see old Harry Hunks and Sacarson.

SIR JOHN DAVYS's Epigrams.

Bear Street, near Leicester Square, was called Bear
Lane in Burridge's *New View of London for* 1708. This was
so called from the Bear and Ragged Staff, the arms of the
Neville and Dudley families.

Bear Lane was the old name for BEER LANE, leading
from Great Tower Street to Lower Thames Street opposite
the Custom House. Stow gives: 'At the east end of Tower
Street, on the south side, have ye Beare Lane, wherein
are many fair houses, and runneth down to Thames
Street.' By the river, near the end of the lane, was Bear
Quay divided later into Great Bear Quay and Little Bear
Quay, appropriated chiefly to the landing and shipment
of corn. Hatton (1708) tells us that market days were
Mondays, Wednesdays and Fridays; and that Bear Key
was between Wiggin's Key and Custom House Key.
Henry III's white bear, a present from Normandy, was
brought here from the Tower, muzzled and chained, and
taken to the river at this spot to catch fish; which imposed

observance of the ceremony upon the Sheriff of London. This seems to be a good reason for the naming of the Lane 'Bear'.

In 1285 a messuage and wharf are described as near the lane called BEREWARDES LANE, so it has been suggested that this lane be identified with that named lane, All Hallows, Barking, one end of which adjoined Tower Street. In 1304 John de Canterbury bequeathed to Hugh, his son, a 'garden' in BEREWARDESLANE in the parish of All Hallows de Berkingechurch; and in 1334 Walter le Milleward left to Katharine, daughter of Henry Swote, fishmonger, 'shops' in Berewardeslane in the parish of All Hallows de Berkingechurch. So there were gardens and shops in this lane.

There was a BERWARDES LANE on the east side of Bishopsgate in the time of Edward I and Edward II. The name was changed to HOG LANE in Stow's time, and ARTILLERY LANE later, which it is now.

Maskell suggests the name of Beer or Bear—either because of the highway to Brewer's Quay, or else from the sign of the Bear there. I do not find Brewer's Quay; and Brewer's Lane (old Grantham Lane) is in Upper Thames Street, some distance away. In the thirty-first of Henry VIII it was called BERELANE (1539). In 1661 the name was spelled Bear Lane, and in 1666 BEERE LANE.

The greatest fire in the city since 1666 began on Thursday, 13 January 1714, in the house of a Mr. Walker, an oilman in Thames Street near Bear Key, occasioned by making fireworks against the King's coming to St. Paul's, which, first taking fire, blew up the house at about 5 p.m., consumed upwards of a hundred houses burning

Harp Lane

from the Thames, all one side of WATER LANE, six or seven houses in Tower Street, the back of all Harp Lane, Trinity House, Baker's Hall, the Vine Tavern and other places of note. A great number of people were killed and smothered in the ruins by blowing up some houses in an attempt to confine the fire.

There were two lanes in London with the curious name of BEAR BINDER LANE. The one in the city, Stow describes as:

From the Stock Market and this parish church east up into Lombard Street, some four or five houses a side, and also on the south side of Wool Church, have ye Bearbinder Lane, a part whereof is in this Walbrook Ward.

This was at the Lombard Street end of St. Swithin's Lane and was the spot at which the 1665 plague made its first appearance in the city. Defoe says in his *History of the Plague*, 'To the great affliction of the City, one died within its walls, in the parish of St. Mary Woolnoth's Church, that is to say, in Bear Binder Lane, near Stock's Market'. It was found, however, upon inquiry, that the Frenchman who lived in this lane was one who, having lived in Long Acre, near the infected area, had removed for fear of the distemper, not knowing that he was already infected. This was in the beginning of May. In 1348 Alice Norton, late wife of Gregory atte Shyre, amongst other bequests, left to Thomas atte Shyre intail 'all her shops in the aforesaid parish and in BEREBYNDERESLANE' for the maintenance of a chantry in the Priory of St. Mary de Clerkenwell for the space of seven years next after her decease.

Earlier than this—in 1341—Simon Bakere, fishmonger,

left to his wife Margery two tenements in the same lane for life.

Large's *Way about London* gives a BEARBINDER LANE as being a continuation to Coborn Road and Tredegar Road, Old Ford. In Rocque's 1763 map the whole of the present Coborn Road and of Tredegar Road was Bearbinder Lane. In the 1854 map only part of the latter road was marked so. It is now all Tredegar Road.

Having dealt with many of the lanes which take their names from animals—cows, bulls, sheep, lambs—let us take the horses. It has been impossible to confine oneself to districts in writing about London Lanes, and though to take them in the haphazard and seemingly irresponsible manner in which it has been done in this volume may give cause for remark on the apparent lack of system, still it has been found the easiest (naturally I would seize upon that!) way out of the difficulty on account of there being so many similar, or very nearly similar, names distributed over so many neighbourhoods. Besides horses, birds, beasts in general and fishes supply a goodly few names. A list of these might be found amusing:

1 Bird Lane	3 Falcon Lanes
2 Chick Lanes	1 Goose Lane
1 Chicken Lane	1 Swan Lane
1 Chigene Lane	1 Old Swan Lane
1 Hen and Chicken Lane	1 Peacock Lane
4 Cock Lanes	1 Wildgoose, or Windgoose,
1 New Cock Lane	Lane
1 Fowl Lane	1 Three Cranes Lane
1 Dove Lane	1 Magpye Lane and
3 Duck Lanes	4 Nightingale Lanes

To come to beasts we have:

2 Bear Lanes
1 Beast Lane
2 Bull Lanes
6 Cow Lanes
2 Red Cow Lanes
1 Dead Donkey Lane
1 Dog Lane
1 Elephant Lane
3 Fox Lanes
3 Greyhound Lanes
1 Hampshire Hog Lane
3 Hart Lanes
1 White Hart Lane

3 Hog Lanes
1 Horse Ferry Lane
1 Horsleydown Lane
1 Horsemonger Lane
1 Lamb Lane
2 Sheep Lanes
3 Mutton Lanes (perhaps inadmissible under the heading)
2 Three Colts Lanes
1 Lion-in-the-Wood Lane
2 White Horse Lanes

For fishes we have but two—one Crab Lane and one Dolphin Lane. There is one Fishmonger Lane and one Angler's Lane. The two latter must have had bad sport or suffer from the surname of Washington.

There was one FROG LANE at Islington, which now embraces Rheidol Terrace, part of Prebend Street, and Popham Road, finishing up at New North Road as of old.

The Clothmakers' Almshouses, erected in 1770, are somewhere along there.

In a map dated 1840 Frog Lane was called Brick Lane —the whole length of it.

Since the digression to Islington has been made, to introduce old Frog Lane, a couple more lanes in that district might be mentioned before proceeding with the horses. This aptly illustrates my difficulty just referred to. Now I stick to a district.

Out of old Frog Lane ran River Lane to the end of Colebrook Road, just past Colebrook Cottage where Charles Lamb lived after leaving his occupation as clerk in the India House. Behind this cottage then, as he wrote to Bernard Barton, was 'a spacious garden with vines (I assure you), pears, strawberries, parsnips, leeks, carrots, to delight the heart of old Alcinous'. River Lane is now St. Peter Street.

Theodore Hook came to Islington to take—with Lamb —a last look at the famous old 'Queen's Head' (pulled down in 1829), then at the corner of Queen's Head Lane (now Street), the next lane to River Lane along Frog Lane. He accompanied Lamb home afterwards. During the evening Lamb proposed a race round the garden, but Hook declined, remarking he could outrun nobody but the constable. Sir Walter Raleigh's name has been connected with the old 'Queen's Head'—a strong wood and plaster building of three lofty storeys, projecting over each other in front, and forming bay windows, supported by brackets and carved figures. The centre, which projected several feet beyond the other part of the building, and formed a commodious porch, to which there was a descent of several steps, was supported in front by caryatides of carved oak, standing on either side of the entrance, crowned with Ionic scrolls. John Rivington, the bookseller, lived next door. In Queen's Head Lane, or Road, is a public-house with the sign of the 'Ram and Teasel', which is a part of the arms of the Clothmakers' Company, whose almshouses are near by. This lane was previously called Almshouse Lane and before that Boon's Lane.

Along Essex Road at 144A, the now Street, by the side

of the public-house which gives its name to it, was once GREENMAN LANE which ran into old Frog Lane just before the latter reached New North Road. The present Essex Street was called Lower Road. The old Essex Street (now Danbury Street) reached from Vincent Terrace to River Lane.

MOTT'S LANE was at the end of Essex Road near its junction with Balls Pond Road, at the end of which latter road the long winding DALSTON LANE commences. George II visited his lady-love, the Baroness de Bode, at a residence he took for her at Nos. 152 and 154, once a single house; afterwards first a girls' and then a boys' school.

HARTWELL'S LANE is given in Large's *Way about London* as being the first on the right in Dalston Lane from Amherst Road East. There is a Hartwell's Road, now, at No. 25 Dalston Lane. Without following this lane to its end at Mare Street, Hackney, we will turn down Kingsland Road (we have been here before in connection with Cock and Castle and Shacklewell Lanes) at No. 372 to the present Haggerston Road, the first part of which is old STONE-BRIDGE LANE. This went as far as Brunswick Street. There HAGGERSTON LANE joined it and completed a winding, almost semi-circular lane, rejoining Kingsland Road at No. 210. These two lanes are together now called Haggerston Road with the exception of the bend turning south again to Kingsland Road. This is renamed Laburnum Street. Why? At the commencement of old Stonebridge Lane are raised and railed pavements, the road dipping between. There are still some old red scallop-tiled cottages on the right with little front gardens opposite the old Stonebridge Green, which is now most beautifully asphalted to kill any lingering idea of a 'lane' with a 'village green' having ever been here.

From old Haggerston Lane nearly due east, some little distance, is Sheep Lane, already mentioned; whence, across Mare Street to Cambridge Heath Station, down Parmiter Street, we come to RUSSIA LANE—quite an uninteresting place of modern cottages. Across OLD FORD LANE (now Road), down GLOBE LANE (also now Road) to Mile End Road, crossing which, bearing slightly left, is White Horse Lane, Stepney—Thomas Burke's 'Street of Beautiful Children'. This lane, in Cruchley's *New Plan of London*, dated 1829, only commenced at Trafalgar Square, now on its left-hand side, and ran into old Cow Lane (now Ben Jonson Road) at the bottom. The top end of the present lane, north of the Square, was there called George Street.

While here we must mention DUCKETT'S LANE, which then ran from Ernest Street to Alfred Street (parallel turnings out of Whitehorse Lane). Since 1829 it has extended itself, and taken in its old continuation to Cow Lane— Edward Street—and is now all called Duckett Street. In 1554–5 John Watson, a parishioner of St. Albans, Wood Street, left 10 marks for mending Duckett's Lane.

THREE COLT LANE is back to Mile End Road, thence left to Cambridge Road; at No. 205 of which, connecting it with London Street by Bethnal Green Junction, is this lane. Three Colt Lane is the old name of the present street of that name from Limehouse Church to Emmett Street.

HORSELYDOWN LANE, Bermondsey, runs from Queen Elizabeth Street to Shad Thames. Horselydown was the old name for a district that extended from the eastern end of Tooley Street to Dockhead, and from the Thames to the Tenter Ground, Bermondsey, now built over, but was formerly a grazing ground for horses. Hence the name.

HORSEMONGER LANE is now called Union Road and runs from Newington Causeway to Falmouth Road (it seems). The recreation ground here now is on the site of the old Horsemonger Gaol, the then county-gaol for Surrey. Almost the last two persons executed for treason, Wm. Cundall and John Smith, being two of fourteen British subjects taken in the enemy's service in the Isles of France and Bourbon, were hanged and beheaded in the lodge of this gaol on 16 March 1812. The Cato Street conspirators were actually the last—in May 1820.

Leigh Hunt was confined here for two years from 1812–14 for a libel on the Prince Regent in the *Examiner* newspaper.

Lord Byron visited him here. In June 1813 Lord Byron and Mr. Moore dined here with him.

Charles Dickens interviewed the executioner of the Mannings outside the gaol on 13 November 1849 and expressed himself 'astounded and appalled' at the wicked behaviour of the masses there congregated.

HORSEFERRY LANE was out of Fore Street, Limehouse. This street was that part of the present Narrow Street between Ropemaker Street and Three Colts Lane and Limehouse Causeway. Out of this last-named lane was a GREYHOUND LANE.

The river end of the present Horseferry Road, Westminster, was once called Horseferry Lane, then Market Street, and after all Horseferry Road. Just round the corner of the old lane, in what is now Grosvenor Road, was to be found a very fine hood over the doorway of No. 9

Grosvenor Road, lately demolished, built in the latter part of the seventeenth century by Sir John Crosse. Afterwards occupied by Mr. Vidler, the Government contractor, this was the house, with stables and courtyard at rear, to which the mail-coaches, before the unromantic days of railroads, were driven in procession, annually, upon the King's birthday. They started from Lombard Street. The first occasion was in 1790; upon which sixteen coaches with plated harness and hammercloths of scarlet and gold started.

From Mr. Vidler's business arose the London Road Car Company, and the General Omnibus Company.

Another Greyhound Lane is given in a map of 1840 running from 221 Whitechapel Road. This is now called Fulborne Street—DUCKING POND LANE (now Road) ran across the bottom. This latter is now part of Outward Street. A recreation ground is now to the west of Fulborne Street. Baker's Lane and Charles Street have been wiped out to form Vallance Road. Greyhound Lane, in the 1829 map, was marked John Street.

A third Greyhound Lane (now Road) runs from Fulham Palace Road to NORMAND (late Lane, now Road), and continues under the name STAR LANE (also now changed to Road) to North End Road.

While in this district I will mention that at Hammersmith, from 227 King Street to New Street, runs HAMPSHIRE HOG LANE, a very picturesque paved lane with old brick walls each side. The Hampshire House Club is here.

OLD HOG LANE at Norton Folgate is now part of Worship Street. In this lane lived the player in Henslowe's company of actors who was killed in a duel with Ben Jonson. His

Doorway
at
No 9 Grosvenor Road S.W.1.

sword was 10 inches longer than that of rare Ben, who was imprisoned and narrowly escaped being hanged. In 1767 the officiating priest of a Mass house in this Hog Lane was condemned to perpetual imprisonment simply for saying Mass and giving communion to a sick person. After four years the sentence was commuted into exile for life.

Another old Hog Lane—afterwards (since 1700) called Crown Street and now part of Charing Cross Road—was built about 1675, in which year it was mentioned by Ogilby. It was still so called in Dodsley's *London*, 1761. On a stone let into the wall of a house at the corner of the then Rose Street was the new name with date 1762. Hogarth laid the scene of his *Noon* in Hog Lane. The background contains a view of the Church of St. Giles's-in-the-Fields. Engravings of this are generally reversed, which makes it seem untrue to locality—which Hogarth never was.

The whole of the east side of the old lane was demolished when the present Charing Cross Road was planned. In 1889 it was being rebuilt at a great rate.

A Hog Lane is mentioned as being at West End, Hammersmith. Hoggenlane was another name for Huggin Lane, Upper Thames Street. In Rocque's map of 1703 HOGMORE LANE is the old name for Gloucester Road, Kensington Gore.

PETTICOAT LANE, now Middlesex Street, was called Hog Lane at one time; as Strype remarks, 'perhaps from the Hogs that ran in the fields there'. He also tells us that in a fine old map of London (some time in the possession of Mr. Pepys of Clapham) he observed only a few scattering houses in this lane; but the east side yet wholly unbuilt and consisting only of fields, where cows and other cattle were

I

feeding. In ancient times it was such a pleasant place with hedgerows on each side and elm trees, in the midst of fields, that some gentlemen of the Court and City built themselves houses here on account of the fine air to be had. Near the Spanish Ambassador's house (Gondomar's) on the east side down a paved alley—Strype Alley, from Strype's father who lived there—was a fair large house with a good garden before it, built and inhabited by Hans Jacobson, the King's jeweller, wherein Strype was born. After many French Protestants fled their country many planted themselves here in that part of the lane nearest Spitalfields, to follow their trade—mostly Broad Weavers of silk—and it soon became a continuous row of buildings on both sides of the way. Then the Jews took possession and the buildings became houses and shops for second-hand clothes, and stolen goods. A few years ago one might have lost a silk handkerchief at one end of the lane, and bought the same article at the other end. The village postman, just returned from a holiday in London during which he visited many parts of it, was wearing a tiepin containing a glittering ——(?)

'Is it a real one?'

'Well! If it ain't, one of those coves that tell the tale in Petticoat Lane has had me for one-and-six!'

It has been suggested that this lane might have taken its intimately familiar title from Petit Court—Little Short Lane. It is not quite the same now as it used to be when every Sunday morning one could buy anything from petticoats to pastries and pickles; from jackets to jewellery—a market kept by the Jews for the Gentiles—one of the main ducts or arteries of Hebrew London, absolutely *sui generis*. Nothing else could be like it on a Sunday! An

Hampshire Hog Lane

entrance from Houndsditch is through HARROW LANE—
now Harrow Alley—a tortuous thoroughfare—the topographical amenities of the lane have much changed. In
Noorthouck's map of 1772 it is called Petticoat Lane; in
Cruchley's *New View of London*, 1829, it is marked Petticoat
Lane, and also in Mogg's 1840 map; but in 1854 it is
called Middlesex Street, and also in an 1895 map. In the
Post Office *List of Principal Streets and Places in London for
1857* it is called Middlesex Street.

Peter Cunningham, in paragraph No. 31 of the Introduc-
tions to his *Handbook of London*, says: 'Hog-lane, Aldgate,
was new-named Petticoat-lane, and is now Rosemary-lane.'
This is the only mention I have found of the latter having
once been a name for Petticoat Lane. He does not mention
this either under the heading of Hog Lane or that of Petticoat Lane. This Hog Lane was the one which at one time
embraced not only Petticoat Lane, but Artillery Lane as
well. This is east out of Bishopsgate Street, part in Bishopsgate Ward without and the other in Stepney. Nos. 2 to 30
and 1 to 23 are within the City Boundary, and form the
site of the Old Artillery Ground, of which the bounds are
set out in letters patent in the time of James II, and shown
in Ogilby and Morgan's map of 1667 as an open space
called Old Artillery Garden—part of the site of the Teazle
Close, which was a field belonging to the dissolved priory
and hospital of St. Mary Spital beyond Bishopsgate, given
by Henry VIII to the 'Fraternity of Artillery'. The charter
was granted in great and small ordnance, but surrendered
in 1585 for a new charter with larger powers during the
year of the Spanish invasion. The City troops mustered in
great strength at camp at Tilbury, when the Captains were

selected from the Artillery Company and called Captains of the Artillery Garden. The danger passed, exercises and assemblies were neglected, and the Artillery Garden was reserved for the practice grounds of the Tower; the site is now marked by Artillery Lane.

The archers were forbidden to shoot there in 1677, according to letters and papers of Charles II, *Domestic Series*, XVIII, p. 533. The members of the Company had removed in 1641 to Finsbury. The inhabitants there petitioned on 19 May 1641, stating that:

The military gentlemen of London are making Suit to have their fields for their military garden, and intend to build a high brick wall about it, to the great inconvenience of those who dwell in the neighbourhood of the Archer, who go out this way to recreate themselves, to the danger of riders whose horses will be frightened by the guns; of travellers who will have no opportunity of escaping thieves, or sextons conveying the plague-stricken to the pest-house, besides the disturbances to the sick and damage to house property. They accordingly pray that the military may be restrained from building the wall and the rights of petitioners be preserved.

> The Teazle-ground—by indenture bearing date,
> January's third day in Henry's time,
> Th' Eighth of that name; the convent did conjoin
> Unto the Guild of all Artillery,
> Cross-bows, handguns, and of archery,
> For full three hundred years, excepting three.

This, written by Petowe, the Company's poet, referred to the fact that the last Prior of St. Mary Spital granted the ground for thrice ninety-nine years.

From about 1610, when Philip Hudson, Lieutenant of the Company, got to work, dates the revival of the Honour-

Artillery Lane

able Artillery Company. On 13 July 1612 there was an Order in Council that the citizens of London be permitted to exercise arms in the Artillery Garden, or other convenient place, provided their number be not more than 250.

In Ogilby's 1677 map, the site of the Old Artillery Garden is shown as well as the new Garden in Bunhill Row.

As an illustration of night-time customs in James I's time, William Carpenter of Artillery lane, chaundler, with another man named Patchet of Carter layne, were bound over in twenty pounds each for the appearance of Joyce Lyde, wife of William Lyde of Fosterlayne, chaundler— she having been 'taken wandering about twelve of ye clock in ye night tyme in ye componie of a young man by ye Watch of Grubstreet'.

My sketch in this lane is of one of the most beautiful old shop fronts in London—still there in the occupation of Mr. Arthur Locke, a grocer. He tells me of a curious fact. Two other fine old shop fronts remaining in London are also connected with a similar name. The famous old hat shop in St. James's Street is 'Lock's' and Freiburg and Treyer's fine old shop in the Haymarket belongs to a Mr. Locke.

Another Artillery Lane at 196 Tooley Street reminds us that the old Artillery Hall of the Southwark 'Trainbands' stood on the site of the present workhouse in Parish Street. The Hall was erected in 1639 when the Governors of St. Olave's Grammar School granted a lease to Cornelius Cooke and others of a piece of ground, forming part of Horseydown, and enclosed with a brick wall, to be employed for a Martial Yard, in which the Hall was built. When Horseydown was built over, about the middle of the seventeenth century, a street of houses, running north to south, near to Dockhead, was called THREE OAK LANE, from three oaks formerly standing there. In 1725 the Artillery Hall was converted into a workhouse, and in 1736 the Parish Church of St. John, Horselydown, was built on part of the Martial ground.

OLD HORSELYDOWN LANE is now MORGAN'S LANE at 113 Tooley Street. In Newcomb's map of 1658 is shown an open space marked Horsy Downe, and adjacent to it the large enclosure of the Artillery Yard.

From the corner of Bermondsey Street to Horsleydown was Horselydown Lane, and here, on the west side of Stoney Lane—once a Roman road leading to the ferry over the river to the Tower—was Sir John Fastolf's mansion. He was Governor of Normandy, and fought at Agincourt: he died in 1460. His mansion was here at the time of Jack Cade's insurrection; when Sir John garrisoned it with old soldiers from Normandy to arrest Cade's progress. Cicely, mother of the Duke of York (afterwards Edward IV), stayed in this house with her family. She owned much property in this neighbourhood, part of which came, by bequest, into the hands of Magdalen College, Oxford, in connection with which fact is the present Magdalen Street, previously MAUDLIN LANE.

Another Stoney Lane runs from 71 Middlesex Street to Houndsditch.

Near the old MILL LANE at 67–69 Tooley Street once stood the House of the Abbots of Battle, called the Manor of Maze, with beautiful gardens and a clear stream flowing down the old lane and turning the Abbot's Mill at Battle Bridge stairs. The lane is now called BATTLE BRIDGE LANE.

Battle Bridge Lane.

The Borough Compter, before removal to St. Margaret's Hill, was in the lane. Until at least as late as 1866 the famous old inn, the 'Red Lion and Key', built in 1651, was also there.

Large, in his *Way About London*, gives a Mill Lane off Blue Anchor Road, Bermondsey, the second turning on the right from Balaklava Road. Mill Lane was the old name of the present Mill Street at St. Saviour's Dock. In the Post Office list for 1881 is a Mill Lane off New Park Road, Brixton. Another Mill Lane is at Shootup Hill, Brondesbury. A MILLER'S LANE is off Upper Kennington Lane.

MAZE LANE, now Maze Pond, was part of the gardens of the mansion of the Abbots of Battle.

CRUCIFIX LANE, off Bermondsey Street, seems by its name to have belonged to the old religious house of St. Mary Overy.

FREEMAN'S LANE was the second on the left in Queen Elizabeth Street, Bermondsey, and ran to the end of Pickleherring Street. It was probably demolished in the formation of the south approach to Tower Bridge. Close by Queen Elizabeth Street is WEAVER'S LANE, out of Tooley Street by Potter's Fields Gardens.

Between 49 and 51 Tooley Street is MAY'S LANE.

EAST LANE at Bermondsey is considerably west of WEST LANE, Bermondsey Wall. Much of the old picturesque lane with its cottages has disappeared. The L.C.C. Schools and the Peabody Trust buildings are not things of beauty.

Between this East Lane and George Road was SALISBURY LANE, identical, in 1840 map, with Flockton Street. Salisbury Street there runs from 191 Jamaica Road to Bermondsey Wall, opposite Fountain Stairs.

Another East Lane is at Poplar, the first turning east of
the King's Road. Yet another East Lane in Old Kent
Road, the sixth on the right below the 'Bricklayers' Arms',
leads to Walworth. An old East Lane, now promoted to
Street, is at about 275 Walworth Road, opposite what is
now called Penrose Street.

Old Rosemary Lane from Sparrow Corner, Minories, to
Cable Street, Whitechapel, was renamed Royal Mint
Street in 1850. This called forth the remark 'Rosemary
lane, a region thus graphically described by Pope in the
Dunciad:

> Where wave the tatter'd fragments of Rag Fair.

Long known as the mart of old clothes, rags and secondary
goods of all sorts, this lane has recently been ennobled
by the appellation of Royal Mint Street'.

Cable Street is the old Back Lane.

Rag Fair—the notorious old-clothes market, was in
Rosemary lane. Tennant says:

> There is no expressing the poverty of the goods; nor
> yet their cheapness. A distinguished merchant engaged
> with a purchaser, observing me to look at him with great
> attention, called out to me, as his customer was going
> off with his bargain, to observe that man, 'For', says he,
> 'I have actually clothed him for fourteen pence'.

At the end of the seventeenth century this Rosemary
Lane contained several music-houses (forerunners of the
music-halls) which became nightly scenes of intoxication,
riots and even murder. In 1699 peace officers made
repeated searches in these, and in one night took into
custody 'about forty couples of suspicious persons, who were

all committed'. That is an extract from the *Protestant Mercury* of 29 March 1699.

In the Burial Register of St. Mary's, Whitechapel, is an entry in 1646: June 21st Richard Brandon a man out of Rosemary Lane. To this is added, 'This R. Brandon is supposed to have cut off the head of Charles I'.

Goldsmith speaks of the pincushion makers in this lane. In a court off it an annotator of Beloc's *Anecdotes of Literature* says he observed in 1807 an ancient sign over the door of an ale-house which was called the 'Four Alls' the figure of a king, and on a label 'I rule all'; figure of a priest, motto —'I pray for all'; a soldier—'I fight for all'; and a yeoman —'I pay for all'. About 1809 he passed up the same thoroughfare and found a painted board inscribed with the words 'The Four Awls'! So it is not the names and meaning of the names of streets only which are liable to change. Rosemary for Remembrance.

A tavern token in the Guildhall, No. 947, has 'Edward Reade in—Fruiterer's Arms, in the field'. Reverse: 'Rosemary Lane—In the field E.T.R.'

The emblazonment on the shield of the Fruiterer's Arms is an apple-tree, the tempter, or serpent, twined about the trunk, presenting the apple to Eve, Adam being on the dexter side.

The subject is generally known as the 'Adam and Eve'. Some pothouse bard (whom 'the Brewer's dog had bitten on the brain') in the days of Charles II wrote:

> All women rightly are called Eves,
>   Because they come from Adam's wife:
> Add thi to eves, and they are thieves,
>   And oft rob men of merry life,

To eve add ls, they are evels,
Let d precede, they are devels:
Thus eves are thieves, thieves are evils,
And angry eves worse than devils.

Building was forbidden in Rosemary Lane in James I's time. According to the Gaol Delivery Rolls, 15 September, 5 James I: On the 29th August, 5 James I—Recognizance, taken before Sir Wm. Wood Kent, Lieutenant of the Tower of London and J.P. of Owen Hove of Whitechappell co. Midd. yeoman, in the sum of ten pounds; for the said Owen's appearance at the next Session of the Peace, and in the meantime for his forbearance from building houses in Rosemary Lane.

Nicholson, in his *New View of London*, 1708, gives a Rosemary Lane, 'on the east side of Pye Corner, a passage to Long Walk, Town Ditch'. The Town Ditch was a broad passage just without the City Wall, between Christ's Hospital and Little Britain, so called from the Ditch that was just without the walls of the City for its better security, over which there were bridges at the several gates and one at this place, as may be seen in Stow's *Survey*. This Ditch about the City was first made in 1213, in King John's reign, 204 feet broad, at the charge of the citizens when Roger Fitz Alwyn was Mayor.

It is interesting to recall the fact that the eastern play-ground of the Bluecoat Boys—a cobbled yard about 90 yards by 50 yards—was always called The Ditch. This had an entrance by the Beadle's lodge through old wrought-iron gates from Little Britain.

CHAPTER VI

GRAY'S INN LANE—THE LANE BY WHICH TOM Jones entered London and put up at the Bull and Gate, Holborn—the lane in which Hampden and Pym lived and in which they held their consultations for resisting the impost of shipmoney— the lane that was once called PORTPOOL LANE, only about 600 yards in length (said Hatton in 1708), which ran from Holborn to King's Road (now Theobalds Road) and Liquorpond Street (now Clerkenwell Road)—is no longer. It has been swallowed up by its old continuation, Gray's Inn Road. But there is still a Portpool Lane, from the now Gray's Inn Road to Leather Lane, between Holborn Hall—not now the Town Hall—and Verulam Street.

Portpool Lane, Gray's Inn, is 'The Manor of Portpoole, otherwise called Gray's Inn and four messuages, four gardens, the site of a windmill, eight acres of land, ten shillings of free rent and the advowson of the Chauntry of Portpoole' transferred in August 1505 by indenture of bargain and sale by Edmund Lord Gray of Wilton to Hugh Denny Esquire.

Dodsley says there was, in 1761, a Welch Charity School here, with fifty boys; no girls.

In Stow's time I expect it was all called Gray's Inn Lane as far as it went before it came to the fields, for he explains that it was so called of the inn of court, named

Grayes, a goodly house there situate, and that the lane was 'furnished with fair buildings and many tenements on both the sides, leading to the fields towards Highgate and Hamsted'.

In Queen Elizabeth's time, one John Thorpe, though he 'put himself Not Guilty' of despoiling Mr. Wm. Crosse of Gray's Inn of his goods, but admitted 'Cul de fracione et intracione cubicule', was sentenced to be whipped in Gray's Inne Lane.

LITTLE GRAY'S INN LANE is off the longer lane just north of Clerkenwell Road.

LEATHER LANE runs nearly parallel with Gray's Inn Road from 128 Holborn to Clerkenwell Road. The extreme south-western corner only is in Farringdon Ward without, the lane lying in the Borough of Holborn.

Stow says: 'Then higher is Lither Lane'—having previously mentioned a Gold Lane. He proceeds 'turning also to the field, late replenished with houses built'.

Strype mentions: 'The East side of this lane is best built, having all brick houses. . . . In this lane is White Hart Inn, Nag's Head Inn, and King's Head Inn—all indifferent.' The two latter remain. The lane traverses a very poor neighbourhood, but improved. From the north end it is really picturesque (as I have endeavoured to show in my sketch) with its stalls, barrows and occasional donkey carts—selling all sorts of vegetables, fruit, fish, tinned delicacies (?), soaps, sweets, old books, new books, bric-à-brac, and all things dear to a cheap market.

In the Court of Hastings Calendar of Wills it is called LOUERONE LANE in 1306; in 1331, LYNEROUNE-LANE; in the fourth of Edward III we first get LIVERONELANE; in

Leather Lane

1353 it changes to LENUR and LEMIR LANE; in the twenty-third of Henry VIII we have LYVER LANE and in 1604 LITHER LANE alias LIVER LANE.

Harben suggests that though the name is now obviously corrupt it may be derived from one of the personal names 'Leofrun' or 'Leueron'.

The GOLDELANE, or GOLD LANE, previously referred to is mentioned in the will of Geoffrey de Chelchehethe, tanner, who bequeaths, in 1314, to his son William, tenements in the parish of St. Andrew de Holeburne in this named lane.

In 1317 GOLDEN LANE in the same parish is mentioned by the testator Roger de Notyngham, who bequeaths nine shops in this lane to his wife Matilda for life.

I find no trace of the name 'Gold' as a lane here. But as Stow says: 'Down Snore Hill to Oldborne bridge and up Oldborne Hill, by Gold lane on the right hand, sometime a filthy passage into the fields, now both sides built with small tenements', and 'Lither Lane beyond it' I conclude it is the same as FIELD LANE, since that lane, Ely Place and Hatton Garden, were the only turnings on the right before coming to Leather Lane. Field Lane was much shortened in the formation of Holborn Viaduct and its approaches, and was a narrow way from the foot of Holborn Hill to Saffron Hill; once one of the most disreputable places in London, inhabited chiefly by thieves and receivers of stolen property. Dickens gives a good description of it as it was in 1837, in *Oliver Twist*:

Near to the spot on which Snow Hill and Holborn meet ... a narrow and dismal alley, leading to Saffron Hill. In its filthy shops are exposed for sale huge bunches of pocket handkerchiefs of all sizes and patterns, for here reside the traders who purchase them from pickpockets. . . . Confined as the limits of Field Lane are, it has its barber, its coffee-shop, its beer-shop, and its fried fish warehouse. It is a commercial colony in itself—the emporium of petty larceny, visited at early morning and setting-in of dusk by silent merchants, who traffic in dark back parlours, and go as strangely as they come. Here the clothes-man, the shoe-vamper, and the rag-merchant, display their goods as sign-boards to the petty thief, and stores of old iron and bones, and heaps of mildewy fragments of woollen-stuff and linen, rust and rot in the grimy cellars.

Old Chick Lane, already described, ran into Field Lane. So dangerous was this neighbourhood, Cunningham says, that in his time, without an escort of policemen in plain clothes, the clergy of St. Andrew's, Holborn, would not visit these purlieus of their parish.

The Earl of Shaftesbury and Mr. W. C. Bevan in their philanthropic labours established the Field Lane Ragged School here in 1842, the Field Lane Industrial School, and the Home for Female Servants. The Field Lane Night Refuge was established in 1851.

Field Lane appears now to be called Great Saffron Hill, with Little Saffron Hill as its northward continuation.

There was another Field Lane, commonly called JACK-AN-APES LANE, described as having been between Chancery Lane and Lincoln's Inn Fields, where now is part of Carey Street. But the London Topographical Society in their *Record*, Vol. X, says it ran between Chancery Lane and Bell Yard, a little below Carey Street, so that precisely defines the position.

About 9 p.m. on 15 April 1680, John Arnold, Esquire,

one of His Majesty's Justices of the Peace for the County of Monmouthshire, going home to his lodgings, was set upon in Bell Yard near Jackanape's Lane by three fellows who dangerously wounded him, endeavouring to cut his throat.

Since we are on the spot, CHANCERY LANE, or CHANCELLOR'S LANE, shall be taken next. I cannot do better than start with old Stow's description:

Beyond this Old Temple and the Bishop of Lincoln's House is New Street, so called in the reign of Henry III, when he, of a Jew's house, formed the House of Converts betwixt the Old Temple and the New. The same street hath since been called Chancery Lane, by reason that King Edward III annexed the House of Converts by patent to the Office of Custos Rotulorum, or Master of the Rolls.

The present Rolls Chapel was built in 1617 by Inigo Jones. Dr. Donne preached the consecration sermon. Bishop Burnet, Atterbury the Jacobite Bishop of Rochester, and Bishop Butler of the *Analogy of Religion* fame, all preached here.

In Edward I's time the lane was so foul and miry that it was barred up by John Briton, Custos of London, 'to hinder any harm that might happen in passing that way', as Strype tells us. The Bishop of Chichester, living in the lane, kept the bar up for many years. He died here in 1244. His memory is perpetrated in Chichester's Rents between Nos. 83 and 84 in the Lane. After his decease, and in place of his house, Henry Lacy, Earl of Lincoln, Constable of Chester and Custos of England, built his Inn, where he died in 1310.

The present Lincoln's Inn is part of the said great house.

During the reign of Henry VIII a great builder in the lane was Sir Thomas Lovell, who built the gate-house, dated 1518, and the forefront towards the east. He placed the Lacy's arms thereon as well as his own.

Until about 1670 the lane had no sewer at all. In a large red brick mansion near old Sergeant's Inn in Charles I's time resided Lord Keeper Guildford. In consequence of the illness of his wife, the cause of which ill health was found to lay in the fact that all the drainage of the house went into a small well in his cellar, from which, when full, a pump went to work to carry it into the open kennel of the lane, he agitated among the inhabitants and owners of houses here to join in the charges of making a drain, or sewer, all along the lane. They strongly resisted this proposal; and it was only after his Lordship's forceful application to the Commissioner of Sewers that it was brought into effect. An order was made in Henry VIII's time for this lane to be paved from end to end. In James I's time the Lord Conawaye of the Savoy was presented 'for sufferinge great store of timber to be layed in Chancerye Lane'.

The Register of St. Dunstan's records the baptism of Lord Strafford upon 13.4.1593 'at the house of his mother's father, Mr. Robert Atkinson, a bencher of Lincoln's Inn' in this lane. One of the founders of the Society of Arts— Defoe's son-in-law, Henry Baker—was also born in the lane, in 1698.

Old Sergeant's Inn here was called Farringdon's Inn until about 1484. In an indenture of the fourteenth century the Inn is referred to as 'Tenementum domini John Skarle', but probably both Skarle and Robert

Faryngdon, who is named in a deed of 1404 and who gave his name to this Inn (to Farringdon Street and Farringdon Ward also), held the Inn for the Judges and Sergeants. Skarle was Master of the Rolls. Faryngdon was a 'Clerk of the Chancery'.

In 1416 there is accounted to the Bishop of Ely a sum of £6 13s. 4d. for the rent and usage of this Inn. Some quarter of a century later it was let to John Hody and other servants of the land. Hody was Chief Justice of the King's Bench in the time of Henry VI, and just before his demise tried and condemned 'a gret and Konnyng man in astronomye', Roger Bolingbroke, for labouring to 'consume the King's persone by way of nygromancie'.

Up to 1758 the Sergeants-at-Law had another Inn in Fleet Street, but in that year the Fleet Street members joined the Chancery Lane Inn, and from that time the whole Fraternity united at these quarters until the Inn came to the parting of the ways with the Order with which it had been connected for some six centuries. Mr. Pickwick, with his Attorney, repaired to Sergeant's Inn in Chancery Lane to procure a writ of 'Have-his-carcase', as Sam Weller called it, before his removal to the Fleet Prison.

Cardinal Wolsey lived in a house at the Holborn end of the lane, on the eastern side. Imagine the scene now, if he were to issue forth from some building, mount his mule, trapped with crimson, the saddle covered with crimson velvet, and, preceded by his two cross-bearers and his two pillow-bearers, all upon horses trapped in scarlet, and four footmen armed with pole-axes, make his way down the lane amid the cries of his bareheaded

K

gentlemen ushers, 'On, masters, before, and make room for my lord cardinal.' From 1627 to 1644 near the west corner of Chancery Lane and Fleet Street lived Izaak Walton, many years before he published his *Compleat Angler*.

The King's Head Tavern, a fine old carved-timber house—taken down in 1799—was at this south-west corner.

There is a token in the Guildhall of this tavern, No. 288. A man, having drunk very hard here, went staggering up the lane and happened to reel within the railings of the pump. He went round there so often that he got tired, and, leaning on the rails from within, asked a passer-by where he was. 'Over against the Chancery,' he was told. 'I thought so,' said he, 'and the reason, I think, I shall never get out of this place.' The Chancery is now the Rolls Court.

Hogarth, in his print *Burning the Rumps*, published in 1726 in Butler's *Hudibras*, has included a view of this tavern. There are fourteen other old tokens of Chancery Lane taverns and establishments in the Guildhall. CONVERT'S LANE was an old name for Chancery Lane, in commemoration of the House of Converts in the Lane, which in Edward III's time was made use of as a Rolls Office.

BALLARDES LANE ran west out of Chancery Lane.

In Fleet Street, a little to the west of the end of Chancery Lane, is a fine red-brick and stone-fronted gate-house, built in 1684 by Wren. The previous gate-house was erected by Wolsey's prisoner, Sir Amias Paulet, as an imposed fine. He decorated it with Cardinal's hat and arms, thinking to appease displeasure. This marks the

entrance to MIDDLE TEMPLE LANE. The Grand Hall has
a fine open-timber roof. The collection of State pictures
comprises all the sovereigns from Charles I to George I
inclusive. That by Van Dyck of Charles I is one of the
finest equestrian portraits in existence, and has hung in
the Hall since 1684. Here was performed Shakespeare's
Twelfth Night. Evelyn condemns the revels here as 'an old
but rioutous custom'.

Elias Ashmole, the antiquary, had chambers in the lane.
In 1679 he lost the library he had been collecting for
thirty-three years (in consequence of a fire which began
in the next chambers), in addition to 9,000 coins, ancient
and modern, seals, charters and other antiquities. For-
tunately his collection of manuscripts was at his Lambeth
house.

INNER TEMPLE LANE, in No. 1 of which Dr. Johnson
lived from 1760 to 1765, leads through a James I gateway
beneath 17 Fleet Street to the Inner Temple. At the
bottom is the fine postern doorway of the Temple Church,
and westward are the cloisters, built by Wren after the
1678 fire, the fire which Titus Oates pretended to the
Council was a 'contrivance'. The Church is one of the
four circular churches built in England after the Templars'
return from the first and second Crusades, the others being
at Cambridge, Northampton, and Maplestead in Essex.

Upon the pavements, 'in cross-legged effigy devoutly
stretched', are figures of Crusaders.

In the Temple Round lawyers were wont to receive
their clients. Beneath the organ-gallery is a marble tablet
to Oliver Goldsmith, who was buried in the ground east
of the Choir in 1774. The organ is Schmidt's masterpiece,

though additions have been made by Byfield and Bishop. It is remarkable as possessing quarter-tones. The musical service here is very fine. Pope and Warburton met for the first time in Robinson's bookshop, which was on the west side of the gateway here.

The first barometers were sold in London by Jones, a clockmaker in the Lane, instructed by Lord Keeper Guildford.

The gentlemen of the Inner Temple were of old famed for their masques, plays, revels and entertainments. Christmas, Hallow'een, Candlemas and Ascension were anciently kept with great splendour in their Hall. Charles II dined there in 1661.

TEMPLE LANE runs from Bouverie Street to Tudor Street.

SHIRE LANE was just inside Temple Bar and divided the city from the shire—hence its name—and turned into Ficquet's Field. Dodsley spells it SHEER LANE. It was called ROGUE'S LANE in the time of James I. In 1845 it was divided into Upper, Lower, and Middle Serle's Place. The present Serle's Street is all that remains. The rest was demolished for the New Law Courts.

One of the oldest licensed houses in the metropolis was the 'Trumpet' in this lane. The first licence for a public-house was granted in 1621. Andrew Marvell, who died in 1678, refers in jest to this old hostelry: 'Even then he sounds at the same time another trumpet than that in Sheer Lane; to horse and hem in the auditory.' LITTLE SHEER LANE, marked in the 1772 map, ran westward from Sheer Lane across SHIP LANE.

There is a SHIRE-HALL LANE at Hendon.

Rogues Lane was the previous name of old RHODESWELL

Milford Lane

LANE (now Road). Rogues Well, and not Rhodes Well, is distinctly given in Rocque's 1763 map, as the name at the old spring there. Another Rogues Lane is marked running north-east of Deptford Road past the Half-way-House.

POT LANE is the next lane along Deptford Road, forming a delta with it and Rogues Lane.

In Deptford Lower Road is WINDMILL LANE. Another of the same name is at Camberwell, a third at Hackney, and a fourth in Whitechapel.

MILFORD LANE is on the south side of St. Clement Dane's Church and leads down to the Embankment, bearing to the east at the bottom towards the Essex Water Gate. Stow in mentioning this lane says, 'but why so called, I have not read yet'.

A mill stood here in the time of James I, and at the bottom were Milford Stairs.

When it was just a lane, Milford Lane divided the boundaries of Essex and Arundel Houses. In the latter, Princess Elizabeth resided for some time, when Admiral Lord Seymour, who had married Catherine Parr, the widow of the then late King, was in possession.

A guest of the Earl of Arundel there was old Parr, who lived to be 152 years of age. Taylor, the water poet, went to visit him and said of him:

> He will speak merrily, laugh and be merry,
> Drink ale, and now and then a cup of sherry.

Hollar, the artist, engraved his now very scarce plate, *View of London from the roof of Arundel House*, while a guest of the Earl here.

The Rectory of St. Clement Danes for many years

stood about half-way down this lane. There Wm. Roger
Bates, Chaplain to both James I and Charles I, and Rector
of St. Clement Danes, died in March 1633 and was buried
in St. Clement Danes.

This lane, in the seventeenth century, was a great place
of hiding for debtors. Richard Broome, in his *Mad Couple
Well Matched*, speaks of the 'Sanctuary of Whitefriars, the
forts of Fuller's Rents, and Milford Lane, whose walls are
daily battered with the curses of brawling creditors'.

An order was made the 1st October, the sixteenth of
James I, touching certain alehouses of St. Clement Danes,
made at Michaelmas General Sessions of the Peace,
Westminster:—

Whereas Credible information hath bene given to the
Court that divers persons accused for murthers and other
heynous and outragious offences has [*sic*] gotten harbour
and as it were taken sanctuarye in the Alehouses and
Victualling Houses in Milford Lane in the pariche of St.
Clement's Danes in the County of Middlesex, there making
their aboade and calling it by the name Barmawdoes, in-
somuch as no officer dare to execute any warrants or enter
any house to arrest the said offenders or any of them. It
is therefore ordered that the Constable of the said pariche
doe forth with signifie unto all and uerie the persons
whose names are under written from keeping of Ale or
Beere within theire said houses or without, and (if) they
or any of them shall notwithstandinge continew their
victuallinge or selling of beere and ale, attache them and
euery of them and by virtue hereof, not expectinge further
warrant, and bring them before some of His Majestie's
Justices, etc. etc.

The *Publick News* of January 1642 records that thirty-
six (Irish) rebels who 'consulted to set the city of London
on fire in vindication of their friends' who had previously

been arrested and sent to Newgate, were seized in a house in Milford Lane.

Punch may almost be said to have had its birth in Milford Lane. The idea for this journal was the joint work of Mark Lemon and Henry Mayhew. The first meeting upon the matter took place in June 1841 at Mark Lemon's house in Newcastle Street. The 'Edinburgh Castle', at the corner of the lane, was the next meeting-place, at which were present Douglas Jerrold, Stirling Coyne, Laudells, Mayhew, William Newman and Archibald Hemming.

Mr. Henry Baylis and Mr. Hodder were present as lookers-on. Mr. Hemming was to be principal artist. It was intended to call the paper 'The Funny Dog', or 'The London Charivari', allusion being made to funny dogs with comic tales. A suggestion being made that the paper, like a good mixture of punch, would be nothing without a fair modicum of 'Lemon!'—

'Capital idea,' said Mayhew. 'Let us call the paper *Punch.*'

The Clan Tartan Room at the 'Edinburgh Castle' is well worth a visit—a unique collection of forty-eight tartans there, that of the Royal Stuart being in the middle, over the fireplace. The old 'Cheshire Cheese', farther down, has been rebuilt, and the quaint old red-roofed buildings down the hill pulled down. My sketch shows these.

On the other side of the lane stood, until 1852, the 'Three Horseshoes', kept by Jerry Hawthorne. After the disappearance of the stone cross which in Edward I's reign stood opposite the Bishop of Worcester's House (where now is Somerset House), at which Manorial Dues were paid over to the Court of Exchequer, these dues were paid over at the 'Three Horseshoes'. Amongst these dues was one of six horseshoes and sixty-one nails for a piece of land in the parish of St. Clement Danes. Before the Strand improvement of the semi-circle was made the lane was slightly longer at the Strand end. On the east side until 1832 stood several very picturesque buildings principally built of timber, with bay windows. There is a drawing of these in the Crace collection at the British Museum.

A little west of Milford Lane is STRAND LANE, next to No. 162A Strand, the entrance being easily missed. This lane is of great antiquity and is mentioned by Stow as a lane, or way, passing under a bridge down to the landing-place on the banks of the Thames, which was a landing-pier for wherries and called Strand-Bridge.

Addison mentions arriving here with ten sail of apricot boats after having touched at Nine Elms for melons consigned to Covent Garden.

The spring bath in which David Copperfield used to go for a cooler when he was engaged to Dora Spenlove, Betty Trotwood's niece, is still in the lane—having been there since the days of the Romans—the walls being layers of brick and thin layers of stucco, and the pavement of similar bricks ($9\frac{1}{2}$ inches long, $4\frac{1}{2}$ inches broad and $1\frac{3}{4}$ thick) resembling those in the City wall. The bath can be traced back to the Danvers (or D'Anvers) family, of Swithland Hall, Leicestershire, whose mansion stood upon the spot. One proprietor, for twenty-eight years, was Charles Scott, Esq. An obituary has:

On the 2nd January 1868 died at Albert Street, Stevenage, Herts, Charles Scott Esqre, 28 years proprietor of the

Strand Lane
from
Approach Road.

Old Roman Bath, Strand Lane, opposite Newcastle Street, Strand.

At one time it belonged to a sea captain, who, while on a holiday, met Mr. Glave of New Oxford Street, and sold it him. Mr. Glave had a bathe in it every morning. After his death, the Misses Glave disposed of it through the exertions of the Rev. W. Pennington-Bickford, who has preserved it for his parish of St. Clement Danes.

This lane has lost its picturesque cottages—Golden Buildings; also a most attractive and popular nautical resort—the Old Ferry House, known by the sign of 'The Lightermen and Watermen's Arms'. It was a small snug hostelry kept by an old Thames veteran, Jacob Tuller, being much resorted to by the crack watermen of the day. Here met Bob Coombes (the unconquered!), Kelly, Tom Chambers, Dick Mortlake, and the ex-champion, Robert Castles, who conquered Time—rowing a thousand miles in a thousand consecutive hours, off Millwall. He was then made coxswain of the Royal Barge; afterwards appointed Ferryman on St. James's Park waters, and died one of Father Thames's most noted men.

CHAPTER VII

WHILE IN THE NEIGHBOURHOOD OF ST. CLEMENT Danes another lane, Dirty Lane, must be mentioned. Diprose says it was (in 1868) in the Parish of St. Clement Danes.

This Parish is divided into two Liberties—the Upper and the Lower. The Upper, which is in the Liberty of Westminster, contains four Wards, viz. Temple Bar, Sheer Lane, Drury Lane, and Holywell Wards. The Lower Liberty is in the Duchy of Savoy, also containing four Wards, Royal, Church, Middle and Savoy Wards. Dirty Lane is given as having been in the Savoy Ward. I am inclined to think it was another name for the present CARTING LANE which runs off the south side of the Strand by the 'Coal Hole', evidently so called by the coal-heavers working on the Thames. The latter place being their favourite meeting-place after having done their carting up the lane, which was thereby made dirty.

DUTCHY LANE was also in the Savoy Ward, on the south side of the Strand just east of Wellington Street opposite between Catherine and Wellington Streets, and took its name from the Duchy of Lancaster.

The Statute 34 and 35 Henry VIII, cap. 12, cites, among other places to be paved and maintained at the expense of those who had lands or tenements adjoining thereto, 'the lane called FOSCUE LANE, from the garden and tenement of the Bishop of Lichfield', as being 'full of pits and sloughs, very perilous and noysome'. The Strand was, of course, not a continued street, but had only few buildings sparingly erected in it.

In 1559 Henry Smith, student of Middle Temple, having committed suicide, Foxe, in his *Book of Martyrs*, remarks upon the fact: 'And thus being dead and not thought worthy to be interred in the churchyard, he was buried in a lane called FOSKEW LANE.' I cannot trace it.

FETTER LANE extends from Fleet Street to Holborn. Stow gives his derivation of its name: Then is FEWTER LANE which stretcheth into Fleet Street by the east end of St. Dunstan's Church, and is so called of fewters (or idle people) lying there, as in a way leading to gardens; but the same is now of latter years on both sides built through with many fair houses. The way in which this name was usually spelled in old documents of Edward III (1363) was FAITOUR or FAYTOUR. In a will dated 1312 of Richard Gladewyn it is spelled FAITERESLANE.

In a will of 1450 mention is made of '1 Cotag "et 38 garden" inter Shoe Lane et FAITERLANE'.

In July 1643 Nathaniel Tomkins was executed at the Holborn end of Fetter Lane for his participation in the plot to surprise the City, organized by Waller.

'Praise God Barebones' and his brother 'Damned Barebones' both lived in the same house in this lane. Dryden is said to have lived in a house which was pulled down in 1887. Tom Payne (author of *The Rights of Man*) lived at No. 77. John Bagford the antiquary was born in 1675 in the lane. The Moravian's Chapel at No. 32 (bought by them in 1738) is, I believe, the only Chapel of the United

Brethren in London. It has memories of Baxter, Wesley and Whitefield. At No. 17 lived the brutal Mrs. Brownrigg who whipped her female apprentice to death. After the coroner's verdict of wilful murder against this she-devil, she absconded, but was apprehended at Wandsworth. On the day of her execution, 14 September 1767, at Tyburn, the crowd was greater than had been remembered since the days of Dick Turpin and Jack Sheppard, several people being seriously injured in the crush.

About thirty years previously, 1733, Sarah Malcolm was executed at the Fleet Street end of the lane for the murder of three women. Hogarth painted and engraved Sarah. The print, for which the Duke of Roxburghe gave £8 5s., is the rarest of Hogarth's portraits.

The picturesque Nevill's Court is being finally demolished at last; for some houses were pulled down in 1911. A queer little turning on the west side of Fetter Lane is Greystoke Place, with wooden wainscoting at the entrance, in which are still cottages with wooden railings on one side and iron, in front, on the other. The Day Training College here is built on the site of part of St. Dunstan's old burial-ground. This court is marked in Rocque's map of 1746 but must be much older. It was formerly called 'Black Raven Passage'.

Trinity Church Passage, on the east side of Fetter Lane, at No. 18 going from Fleet Street, was once named FEATHER-BED LANE.

Near the Holborn end of Fetter Lane stood the old 'White Horse', whence formerly started the Oxford and West Country stage coaches and waggons. It was at this hostelry that Lord Eldon when he came to town in 1766 met his brother, afterwards Lord Stowell. From here he was taken to see the play at Drury Lane. Coming out it rained hard, and, as there were then but few hackney-coaches, they both got into a sedan chair. Turning out of Fleet Street into Fetter Lane their chairman had an argument with some persons as to who should pass first, with the result that the chair was upset and its occupants soused in the mud.

On the west side of the lane is the New Record Office, finished about 1870 and built to contain the national archives previously deposited in the White Tower, the Chapter House, Westminster Abbey, the Rolls Chapel in Chancery Lane, Carlton Ride in St. James's Park and the State Paper Office, St. James's Park.

Here is to be seen the Domesday Book, a long series of royal charters from the reign of King John, early year-books, great rolls of the Pipe and various documents of unequalled historical value and interest. For the require-ments of the Rolls building, an old tavern, the 'Falcon', was destroyed but rebuilt on the opposite side, dropping the width of one house, nearer to Fleet Street. A token is extant of this. No. 456. Robert Langley at the—A falcon with expanded wings. Reverse: In Fetter Lane—in the field R.I.L.

Another Token is No. 463 of Robert Redway at ye— Lion rampant, in the field—Red Lion in Fetter Lane— His Halfepeny refers to the house which, according to Captain Bedloe in his Narrative of the Popish Plot, 1679, the Papists attempted to set on fire in 1670. He embodies the depositions on oath of the men who attempted that.

Towards the Holborn end of Fetter Lane were some of the oldest chambers of Barnard's Inn.

The next lane on the north side of Fleet Street to Fetter Lane is SHOE LANE, the earliest mention of which in the City records was in 1310, the fourth of Edward II, wherein it is called 'SCOLANE in the Ward without Ludgate'. Mr. W. J. Loftie in his *History of London* refers to the 'outlying suburb of SHOWELL LANE, now Shoe Lane'.

In 1345 Thomas de Doningtone was condemned to be hanged for stealing one furred surcoat and two double hoods, value four shillings, and two linen sheets, value forty pence in 'SHOLANE near Holbourne'.

In a roll of 48 Edward III Bangor House, in this lane, south of St. Andrew's Church, is described as the palace of the Bishops of Bangor. Here was their residence until the time of Charles I.

The Cromwell Parliament's journals mention that Sir John Barkstead, Knight, in 1647, purchased of the trustees for the sale of Bishop's Lands the reversion of a messuage with the appurtenances situate near Shoe Lane, called Bangor House, after a term, for years then unexpired, with some waste ground in length 168 feet and breadth 164 feet, intending to build upon it.

The last Bishop of Bangor to reside there was Bishop Dolben (d. 1633). Bentley's printing offices occupied the site. Mean dwellings were erected upon the grounds, but a garden with lime trees and a rookery remained for a long time until the last of the mansion, octangular or two-storied, was demolished in 1828; being kept in memory by 'Bangor House' and by 'Bangor Court', opposite which

Shoe Lane

were some remains of 'Oldborne Hall', according to Stow 'letten out in divers tenements'.

In the seventeenth century a noted cockpit was in the lane; which lane was then a great centre for designers of broad sheets and rude woodcuts which figured at their heads. The sign-painters also congregated here, and Harp Alley, off the lane, was the great mart for ready-made and second-hand signs.

A noted tavern in Shoe Lane was the 'Ben Jonson', with the poet's head for a sign.

The northern half of the lane was much changed when Holborn Viaduct and its approaches were constructed, and by the clearing away of old Farringdon Market. The new market caused the removal of the burial-ground of St. Andrew's Workhouse in which were buried the remains of Chatterton, the poet. Over the gateway to this work-house was a bas-relief of the Resurrection, a representation of which is at the Church of St. Giles-in-the-Fields. In the *Gentleman's Magazine* for 1816, representations of this are said to be also at St. Dunstan's-in-the-East, and St. Stephen, Coleman Street. Under title 'Ancient Sculptures in the Metropolis' in the same magazine for 1822 the one at St. Giles-in-the-Fields is said to have been set up in 1686 and to be worked in brass! It does not look like brass.

Shoe Lane is associated with four poets: Chatterton, already mentioned; Henry Neele, whose remains lie in St. Andrew's Churchyard; Richard Lovelace, the cavalier poet who died in 1658 in Gunpowder Alley; and Richard Boyce, who died in 1749 in a wretched lodging-house just off the lane. Evans, the astrologer, also lived in Gun-powder Alley.

Opposite the end of the lane was the famous Fleet Street Conduit.

On the south side of Fleet Street at No. 67 was WATER LANE (now Whitefriars Street). The name was changed by the consent of the Commissioners of Sewers and at the request of freeholders in the lane. Here, in excavating for a new sewer, the workmen came upon the foundation of the wall believed to have formed the eastern boundary of the Monastery of the White Friars, founded by Sir Richard Gray in 1241 on ground given by Edward I. At one part of this wall, where they tunnelled through it, two human skulls were found at a depth of about fourteen feet; several bones and some pieces of money. This was a very solid wall composed of flint, brick, slate and granite mixed with mortar. It extended from the river nearly to the top of Water Lane, as it was then called. It was re-named on 5 November 1844.

The foundation wall of the Monastery had been previously found at the corner of this Lombard Street—possibly so named by the 'Alsatians' who flourished here from 1608 to 1696 (see *Fortunes of Nigel*) and made a privileged sanctuary of the district from Fleet Street to the Thames, and from the western side of Water Lane to the Temple.

On the left of the lane is Crown Court, in which until about five years ago was a very old and quaint hostel from which the court took its name, and against the continuous licence of which no complaint had been made for over 200 years. On the right of this court is the famous—or infamous—Hanging Sword Alley, immortalized by Dickens as the place in which Jerry Cruncher lived, and the odd-job man at Tellson's Bank, Temple Bar (Child's). The houses here had a double means of flight—into Water Lane as well as into the Alley with the bloodthirsty name—not to mention the flight of steps at the bottom which could have been taken with a jump. Not only did Dickens give this place a bad name but Hogarth made it his scene in Plate 9 of his Idle and Industrious Apprentices, which shows the betrayal here of Tom Idle returned from sea. The woman is seen receiving the price of it from the leader of the posse. The 'Blood Bowl House' here was a place of the wickedest reputation. And at the bottom of the steps is a little back way leading into Salisbury Square rejoicing in the innocent name of Primrose Hill.

Chronicler Stow tells us, 'Then is Water Lane, running down by the west side of a house called the Hanging Sword to the Thames.' So that probably is the origin of the name of this alley of perilous adventure.

In Stow's *Survey of London*, 1598 (Thomas's edition, p. 148):

King Edward I gave to the prior brethren of that house (White Friars) a plot of ground in Fleete Street, whereupon to build their house, which was since re-edified or new-built by Hugh Courtenay Earl of Devonshire, about the year 1350, the twenty-fourth of Edward III. John Lutken, Mayor of London, and the commonalty of the city granted a lane called CROKER'S LANE reaching from Fleet Street to the Thames, to build in the west of that church.

This is the only mention I find of this lane.

Another Water Lane is at Blackfriars from Broadway to Queen Victoria Street. In this lane is the Dispensary and Hall of the Incorporated Society of Apothecaries, erected in 1670.

The Grocers and Apothecaries were for eleven years

L

one company until James I, at the hint of his own apothecary, Gideon Delaime, granted a charter of Incorporation
to the Apothecaries as a separate and distinct company.

In 1687 a controversy started between the College of
Physicians and the Apothecaries Company. The latter,
'taught the art by doctors' bills to play the doctors' part',
added prescribing to compounding. The Physicians had
the best of an action they brought against an apothecary
named Rose for attending a butcher. This decision was
reversed by the House of Lords in 1703, since when it
has been the law of the land that apothecaries may advise
as well as administer.

In this Water Lane is PRINTING HOUSE LANE, the
passage in 1708 to the Queen's Printing House and thence
to Puddle Dock Hill.

Playhouse Yard is also off this Water Lane. It is part
of the site of the old Blackfriars Theatre built in 1576
by James Burbadge. In 1596 William Shakespeare and
Richard Burbadge were sharers in it. It was pulled down
in 1655 and tenements built on the site.

The Water Lane in Great Tower Street was formerly
called SPORIAR LANE, renamed Water because 'it runneth
down to the watergate by the Custom House in Thames
Street'. The bend part of it in Noorthouck's map of 1772
is marked 'Oram's Court'. The lane is on the site and
part of the Old Trinity House which was burned down in
the Great Fire, again in 1718, and each time rebuilt.
Merchant offices at No. 5 now called the Old Trinity House.
Sir Marmaduke Rawdon, a great merchant during the
reigns of James I and Charles I, had a house in the lane.

There is a Water Lane at Brixton from the Hill to

Dulwich Road, and another one at Stratford. Yet another one at Mill Street, Rotherhithe Wall. Dodsley gives a WATERHOUSE LANE at Shadwell, and a WATERMAN'S LANE at Whitefriars. In the *London Street Directory for* 1881 is a Waterman's Alley, Temple Street, Whitefriars, probably the same. In Larwood's and Hotten's *History of Signboards* WILDERNESS LANE, Dorset Street, Fleet Street, is mentioned in connection with the sign 'The Lion-in-the-Wood'.

Nearly opposite Shoe Lane is BRIDE LANE (at 97 Fleet Street) in which is the ancient St. Bride's Well, over which there was a pump. Cogers' Hall, where the Cogers met from 1756, was held in a tavern here. Curran, Daniel O'Connell and Judge Keogh were members.

Bridewell, the King's House of old time, was in Bride Lane, and until 1225 the Courts were kept in the King's House. Henry VIII built there a fine house for the reception of the Emperor Charles V, who in 1522 was lodged himself at the Black Friars, but his nobles in their new-built Bridewell. In April 1553 the King sent for Mayor Sir George Baron and presented him, for the commonalty and citizens (according to Stow), with Bridewell Palace to be a workhouse for the poor and idle persons of the city, and with seven hundred marks, land and all bedding and other furniture of the House of Savoy, towards their maintenance.

Strype says:

Bride Lane cometh out of Fleet Street by St. Bridget's Churchyard, which, with a turning passage by Bridewell and the Ditch side, falleth down to Woodmonger's Wharfs, by the Thames. This lane is of note for the many hatters there inhabiting.

A turning is shown here in Aggas's 1560 map. A token of William Adley, 1663, in Bride Lane, and another of Daniel Birtwistle, at the White Bear there in 1666, are extant. The Cogers had a meeting-place here at No. 15, 'Cogers' Hall'. The Madrigal Society held their meetings in 1741 in this lane.

In an old Directory for London a Bride Lane is given as being in Little Peter Street (Westminster).

From Water Lane, Blackfriars, to Old Change runs CARTER LANE. In the time of Edward IV there was no thoroughfare through St. Paul's Churchyard; the gates at either end were only opened when the King came in or went out. The people had to go by way of Carter Lane and Broadway to Ludgate. The lane was once called Shoemaker's Row. Hence the reference in *Tarlton's Jests*, by Halliwell: 'In Carter-lane dwelt a merry cobler who, being in company with Tarlton, askt him what countryman the divell was: quoth Tarlton, "A Spaniard, for Spaniards, like the divell, trouble the whole world." '

The western part of the lane was once called GREAT CARTER LANE and the eastern LITTLE CARTER LANE.

In Bell Yard, off the lane, was the inn of that name from which (Peter Cunningham tells us), in 1598, Richard Quyney directed a letter, 'To my loveing good ffrend and countryman, Mr. William Shackespere deliver these', the only letter addressed to Shakespeare known to exist, and which was in possession of Mr. R. Bell Wheler, of Stratford-upon-Avon.

At the 'Hart's Horn' in this lane the Guy Fawkes conspirators held meetings.

Another Carter Lane was in Tooley Street, near St.

Carter Lane.

Olave's Church, in which lane was—till it was pulled down in 1830 to make room for the approaches to the new London Bridge—the Anabaptist Meeting House. The house of the Prior of Lewes was also here.

Out of the previously mentioned Carter Lane are CREED LANE and Sermon Lane. Creed Lane has also been mentioned before. It was, in 1386, known as SPORENERESLANE, and as Sporyer Row in the time of Henry VI and Edward IV, from the spur-makers dwelling there. In Queen Elizabeth's reign it was renamed Creed Lane from the text-writers who at that time lived there, and wrote and sold all sorts of books then in use, namely the A B C with the Paternoster, Ave, Creed, Graces, etc.

The first edition of Spenser's *Shephearde's Calendar* was 'printed and sold by Hugh Singleton dwelling at the signe of the Gylden Tunne, in Creede Lane, neere unto Ludgate'. James Stuart, artist and architect, author of *Antiquities of Athens*, was born in the lane in 1713.

Under Passages to be Improved and Enlarged pursuant to Act of Parliament in 1760, we find 'such part of the houses in Creed Lane to be pulled down as are necessary to widen the passage to 30 feet'.

Sermon Lane runs from 13 Carter Lane to Knightrider Street. This and two others of the same name have already been described after Salmon's Lane.

Crossing Cheapside next to Foster Lane (previously described) is GUTTER LANE, which runs to Gresham Street. This lane was the home of the old goldbeaters, called after 'Guthurun', some time owner thereof. In Walter de Kingeston's Will of 1258 he left his house in GODRONELANE to be sold.

In 1280 Gregory de Rokesley, Mayor of London, chief director of the Royal Mint, ordered the silver of the new coinage then progressing to be of the fineness 'commonly called silver of Guthron's Lane'. The Assay office, Goldsmiths' Hall, is at the northern end of the lane.

Robert de la More in 1284 left to his son Deodatus (Theodore) his house and shops in GODERONESLANE and to his son William his house in GODERESLANE [*sic*] with shop in Westchep, on condition that he teach his brother his trade, and sit with him in his shop whilst being taught, without payment.

In a will of Henry de Ennefend, orbatur, i.e. goldbeater, dated 1291, this lane is spelled GODRENELANE. William de Blith, saddler, in his will, 1351, spells it GOTHERLANE. GOSTER LANE is the spelling in a MS. Chronicle of London in the reign of Edward IV. Robert de Piphurst, goldsmith, seems to have been the one who spelled GUTHURUN, after the owner, nearest, for in his will of 1312 he had GUDRUNLANE.

Fine specimens of Roman pottery have been found here. In Goldsmiths' Hall is a Roman altar with a full-length figure of Apollo, in relief, found on digging the foundations.

Off Gutter Lane runs Huggin Lane (already mentioned in connection with Huggin Lane, Upper Thames Street) and CAREY LANE. My sketch of Gutter Lane shows a corner of each of them on opposite sides.

I can find no history of Carey Lane. Stow spells it KERY LANE.

There was in the thirteenth century a Thomas Carey or Cray who was then Marshall of the Conduit.

Gutter Lane

Opposite Gutter Lane in Gresham Street is STAINING
LANE, as Stow remarks, 'of paper-stainers dwelling there'.
Upon the occasion of Charles V visiting England and
accommodation being requested, the inventory of the signe
of the Egle in Stanyng Lane was returned as having
'VI beddes and a stable for XVI'.

The old church of St. Mary Staining was opposite the
end of the lane, in OAT LANE. The churchyard is still
there. In 1272 Philip Godchep left his house in STANNYNGE-
LANE to be sold to the highest bidder for distribution of
pittances to the infirm lying in the Hospital of St. Bartholomew's and New Hospital, London.

Oat Lane runs from 11 Noble Street to 94 Wood Street,
mentioned in 1666 as OATE LANE. In Rocque's map the
east end is narrower than now and is called Sheers Alley.
Bull's Head Passage, according to Lockie, 1810, was west
out of Wood Street at No. 94, opposite Love Lane, leading
into Oat Lane and Noble Street. The Bull's Head public-
house is still at No. 94, so it seems that the eastern end of
Oat Lane was then called Bull's Head Passage.

LILYPOT LANE is at 7 Noble Street, west out of Staining
Lane, so named from the tenement called Lyllye Potte.
This was situate north of St. John's Alley, in the parish
of St. Leonard, Foster Lane, in 1541, according to the
Calendar of Letters and Papers, Henry VIII, XVI, 243.

The next lane in Cheapside to Gutter Lane is HONEY
LANE—opposite Bow Church. Stow says it is so called
'not of sweetness thereof, being very narrow and somewhat dark, but rather of often washing and sweeping to
keep it clean'. All Hallows' Church was here before the
Fire—not rebuilt; the ground on which it stood was con-

verted into Honey Lane Market, the smallest market in London, removed in 1835. It was famous for the goodness of its provisions. A famous old eating-house—the best pig-ordinary in London—was in Honey Lane. It was called 'The Pig and Beehive'—the latter on account of its situation. In All Hallows' churchyard was buried John Norman, draper, and Mayor of London in 1453. He was the first Mayor who was rowed to Westminster by water; before then they rode on horseback.

In 1287 Richard Honylane left his two shops in the parish of All Hallows' in Honey Lane to be sold for pious uses.

Might not the lane have been named after him?

Opposite this lane, in Cheapside, was the Standard, where criminals were executed, and from which spot, to do penance for witchcraft, walked barefoot to St. Paul's, Eleanor Cobham, wife of Humphrey, Duke of Gloucester, nearly 500 years ago. She was covered with a white sheet and held a taper in her hand. A Honey Lane ran from Richmond Road to Fulham Road, the eastern boundary of what is now Brompton Cemetery. Ifield Road is its present name.

Lawrence Lane is the next lane to Honey Lane and has been already described after Laurence Pountney Lane. IRONMONGER LANE is the next lane, west from Lawrence Lane, in Cheapside. It is spelled ISMONGERELANE in a Coroner's Roll of 1276–7 on the occasion of a murder of a taverner there by his servant Roger de Westminster, and YSMONGERELANE in a will of Henry de Hereford, dated 1286. Dr. Johnson's stepson, Joseph Porter (died 1749) lived here. He was a great friend of Hogarth, who painted his portrait, and spent much time with him here.

Lawrence Lane

Alderman Boydell (d. 1804), the eminent publisher of engravings and patron of engravers, lived at his shop No. 90 Cheapside at the corner of Ironmonger Lane. He was said to issue forth each morning at five o'clock and go to the Pump in the lane, place his wig on its top and sluice his head. He was Lord Mayor in 1790 and one of the last men to wear an 'Egham, Staines and Windsor', i.e. a three-cornered hat.

Nicholas de Renham Edmund, in 1326, bequeathed to his daughter intail all the tenements he acquired from William le Sautryour in ISMONGERNE LANE. A William de Sautreour, a player on the psaltery, was minstrel to Margaret, Queen of England.

The small Church of St. Martin Pomeroy, destroyed in the Great Fire and not rebuilt, was in the lane.

St. Margaret's Rectory, also in the lane, is built on the site of St. Olave, Jewry, the tower of which forms part of the house, which has been acquired to form a central church house for London's youths. This will provide accommodation for much of the organization of the London Division of the Church Lads' Brigade, numbering about 4,000 boys, and for the various fellowships, clubs, and camp movements, which deal with both boys and girls.

In Richard II's reign Roger Clerk of Wandelesworth was attached in the Chamber of the Guildhall to make answer as to Roger atte Hacche who lived in Ironmonger Lane, and who charged him that whereas no physician or surgeon should intermeddle with any medicines or cures within the Liberty of the City but those who are experienced in such arts, he pretended to cure Roger's wife. Roger parted with twelve pence in part payment of a larger sum should she be cured. The cure took the form of a piece of parchment (with nothing on it, as was afterwards discovered) rolled in a piece of cloth of gold, hung round her neck.

She got worse. Curious!

The Court told Roger Clerk that a straw beneath her foot would have been of just as much avail. Which he had to admit. Men who were ready to perjure themselves as false witnesses in those days went about with a straw sticking out from below the foot and shoe—'men of straw'.

Roger Clerk's punishment was quaint. He was to be led through the middle of the City with trumpets and pipes (forerunner of Sequah's processions?), he riding on a horse without a saddle, the said parchment and a whetstone for his lies being hung about his neck, an intimate domestic utensil also being hung before him, and another similar bedroom article on his back.

Next to Ironmonger Lane is Old Jewry, the ancient Colechurch Street, COLCHIRCHE LANE, at the south-west corner of which stood the church of St. Mary, Colechurch, named from its founder, of the name of Cole. The building was constructed upon a vault, above ground, so that there was an ascent of several steps to the church. Two lanes were in Colechurch Street: the one next the church and one further up. In the Calendar of Wills, Court of Husting, London, under date 1323, 11th June, Richard de Gloucestre bequeathed to Johanna his daughter, a nun of Berkyngge, and to Idonea, his daughter, a nun of St. Elena, certain rents of a tenement in the parishes of St. Mary de Colcherch and St. Pancras, between a lane called BORDHAWE and a lane called GROPECOUNTELANE. The

Ironmonger Lane

latter was next the church—Frederick's Place now, so called after Sir John Frederick, Lord Mayor in 1662, who built a stately mansion here, after the Great Fire, afterwards used as the Excise Office. This taken down, the site was formed into a court of very elegant buildings. Newcourt's *Repertorium* says:

Dr. Hibbert, on 5 March 1671 leased out to Sir John Frederick, Knt., for the term of forty years, at £4 per annum rent, reserved to himself and his successors, a toft of ground abutting upon the churchyard on the west on which he built a dwelling house.

In the will dated 10 March 1348, of Thomas de Burton, mercer, he left to John Howle, draper, a tenement and shop in GROPECOUNTELANE in the parishes of St. Pancras and St. Mary Colchirche.

Between 1293 and 1294 Thomas le Batour de Lodingeberi bequeathed to his son Thomas rents in COLCHIRCHELANE, in the parishes of St. Olave's in Colchirch Lane and St. Michael de Bassieshawe.

This church of St. Mary must have been very ancient. In 1275 Hugh de Rokingeham bequeathed to his sons shops in this Bordhaghe (la) in the parish of St. Mary de Colcherch and St. Pancras. Thomas à Beckett and St. Edmund were baptized there. It was not rebuilt after the Fire. As far back as 1279 Henry de Edelmeton (in margin 'Henry Abel') bequeathed to his brother Robert twenty shillings annual rent in GROPECONTELANE. The name is found also in a lease of property in Wells, co. Somerset, dated A.D. 1263, and also in a grant of a somewhat later date (Brit. Mus., Add. Ch. 25,903, 25,904); called GROPE LANE in Roll 70 (50) and understood still to exist as

GRAPE LANE. There was a GROPING LANE off Tower Hill. In *Wonderful Strange News from Wood Street Counter*, 1642: 'It is worse than Pickthatch, Covent Garden, Groping Lane, Tower Hill, St. Giles-in-the-Fields, Bloomsbury, Drury Lane, Westminster or the Bankside.'

In 1305 William de Bettone bequeathed to Henry de Rokingham rent in the parish of St. Mary de Colcherch near BORDHAWELANE for life. This lane was also called BURDELLANE and BORDHANGLY LANE. One explanation given is that it was probably named as it was from a board or timber yard, but that its proximity to the other lane in Colechurch Street suggests a connection with 'bawd'.

The house, or rather the site, at the north corner of Old Jewry has had a curious history. First it was a Jews' Synagogue; then a home for Friars; next a nobleman's house; after that a merchant's house in which mayoralties were kept; and finally a wine-tavern, which it is to the present day. The Friars De Penitentia Jesu Christi, or 'Fratres Sacca' (Friars apparelled in sackcloth) who had already got permission from Henry III to remove from their house near Aldersgate without the gate in SAKFRERE-LANE to any other place, took over this suppressed Jews' Synagogue. In 1305 Robert Fitzwalter obtained possession of the house. In 1439 Robert Large, mercer, kept his mayoralty there, as did Hugh Clopton, mercer, in 1492. Then it became a tavern with the sign of a windmill, says Stow.

In 1259 one William de Colecestre, clerk, left to those Brethren of the Penance of Jesus Christ a dovecot with pigeons.

Sakfrerelane is mentioned in the will of Alan Under-

Seething Lane

wode, cordwainer, as being the place of limit from his tenement of a flow of water, underneath his shops, which he wished to save to Johanna his wife, having bequeathed the said shops to his daughter.

The present Queen Street, Cheapside, was the old SOPER, SOPAR, or SOPERESLANE, which lane, as Stow is careful to explain, took its name 'not of soap-making, as some have supposed, but of Alen le Sopar, in the ninth of Edward II'. That would have been in 1316. Since, in 1283, Adam de Bernelee left to his wife Heliwysa his messuage in the parish of S. Michael de Bassieshawe, also shops in SOPERESLANE, etc., etc., the lane was in existence and so named earlier than Stow states.

An even earlier will was that of Nicholas Bath who in 1259 left rents in Soperslane to his wife.

The lane was rebuilt in 1666 and renamed Queen Street in honour of Catherine of Braganza. A tavern token in the Guildhall Museum rather bears this out—'Will. Clerke at Ye [Cock and Sackbottle] in Soper.' Reverse: 'Lane, alias Queen Street—his halfpeny 1669.'

Joustings were held in West Chepe Street between SOPER's LANE and the great cross in the time of Edward III—one notable one on 21 September 1331. The last wooden shed or shop, with Solar over it, remained at Soper's Lane end, where an old woman sold seeds, roots, and herbs.

The lane was inhabited by pepperers (from which fraternity the modern Grocers' Company arose) until they went to Bucklersbury during the reign of Henry VI, and the cordwainers and curriers replaced them.

John Hammond, pepperer, in 1348, made a bequest of

sixty shillings for clothing for the porters of this lane, and to each of the said porters and to every other labourer in the lane connected with testator's business, twelve pence. In Henry III's time two of the Pepperers became Mayor of London.

From 82 Queen Street runs PANCRAS LANE, probably so called to commemorate the ancient church of St. Pancras which stood on the north side of it before the Great Fire. The cemetery still remains here, also that of St. Benet Sherehog.

That portion of Pancras Lane to the west of SISE LANE was called NEEDLER'S LANE in 1415. The eastern part was called Pencritch (Pancras) Street, and later in 1435, it was known as GOLDHOPER LANE.

The parish church of St. Pancrate (as Stow spells it) was in the old Needler's Lane part. He described it as a proper small church, but divers rich parishioners therein, and hath had of old time many liberal benefactors, but of late, such as, the least bell in their church being broken, have rather sold the same (Justices were charged by Queen Elizabeth to punish such as sold the bells from their churches) for half the value than put the parish to charge with new casting.

Another Pancras Lane has been promoted to Pancras Road. This runs from King's Cross to King's Road, Camden Town. The length of this was given in the 'correct admeasurement of the streets', dated 1801, as being 4 furlongs 31 poles, FIG LANE being mentioned as the last turning off it, and 23 poles from King Street. This would be the present Crowndale Road, the turning before King Street.

Sise Lane has been named as a turning out of the first mentioned Pancras Lane. Peter Cunningham says this is a corruption of ST. SITH'S LANE or ST. OSYTH'S LANE, from the before-mentioned church of St. Benet Sherehog or Syth, destroyed in the Great Fire.

Stow explains that this small church of St. Sith has also an addition of Bennet Shorne (or Shrog or Shorehog), for he had read of it by all these names; but that the most ancient was Shorne, sometime a citizen and stock-fish-monger of London, a new builder, repairer or benefactor thereof, in the reign of Edward II. So that Shorne is but corruptly called Shrog, and more corruptly Sherehog.

SYTHING LANE was, as Stow says, the corrupt spelling for SIDON LANE, but gives no reason. This is the present SEETHING LANE (running from 53 Great Tower Street to 33 Crutched Friars).

In William de Burgoyne's will dated 1258 the lane is spelled SYVIDLANE. In the city records for 1281 it is referred to as SIEUTHENESTRATE or SUIETHENESTRATE.

In 1381 the Mayor and Aldermen of the City granted to Sir Robert Knolles (who took a great part in the suppression of Wat Tyler's rebellion) and Constance his wife, leave to make a hautpas of the height of 14 feet from the west side of their house to the east side of a house also belonging to them beyond SYVEDEN LANE. An annual payment of a red rose was the consideration.

Sir Francis Walsingham lived in this lane and died there in 1590.

In Pepys' time the Navy Office was in the lane. He lived there during the period over which his Diary extends, from 1660–1669. The Three Tuns Tavern, in which he tells us the two brothers Fielding fell out and one killed the other, has disappeared, but tokens are existent of the Pied Dog public-house in the lane, dated 1667.

St. Olave's Church stands at the north-west corner. Pepys, his wife and his brother Tom are all buried there. My sketch shows the gate (to the churchyard) adorned with five skulls, and a formidable display of chevaux-de-frises.

From 67, Great Tower Street to 55 Fenchurch Street is the extent of MARK LANE, in which is situate London's great Corn Market. MART LANE was the original name. In a Coroner's Roll of 1276 it is thus spelt with a final 'e'.

The lane was once known as Blanch Apleton after a manor belonging in the reign of Richard II to Sir Thomas Roos of Hainelake. On the east side of Mark Lane was a court named Blind Chapel Court, a corruption of the name of the manor.

At the Fenchurch end of the lane was All Hallows' Staining Church, called Stane Church (for stone), most of the city churches at this time having been built of timber It nearly all fell down in 1671.

Queen Elizabeth attended service here on her release from the Tower in 1554 and dined on pork and peas afterwards at the 'King's Head', Fenchurch Street, where the metal dish and cover used by her were long preserved. This was one of the four churches in which James II's Second Declaration of Indulgence was read.

The lane by the side of the churchyard—now Star Alley—was called CRADOCK'S LANE in the twelfth or thirteenth century; then Church Alley, till the body of the church was pulled down to enlarge the Clothmakers' Hall; whose Company is bound to keep the old tower of the

church in repair. The Churchwarden's books are in per-
fect order as from 1491, and are full of interesting facts.
In 1492 the great beam light of the church was mentioned
as weighing more than 40 lb., and cost 1*d.* the lb. In 1587
the ringers were paid 1*s.* for ringing the bells at the execution of Mary, Queen of Scots. In 1606 1*s.* was paid for
painting three red crosses on doors of houses infected with
the plague.

The church tower still remains in a small churchyard
at the rear of a house. A mediæval house called Cokedon
Hall stood at the south-west end of the lane. This belonged,
in 1316, to Thomas de Boloigne, who left it to be sold for
pious uses.

In a London Street Directory (it seems for 1881) a
MARK HOUSE LANE is given as being in Lea Bridge Road.

MARKS LANE was the old name of Mack's Road, Southwark Park Road, Bermondsey.

The present Market Street, St. James, was called
MARKET LANE before the Opera Arcade was erected and
the lane ran from Jermyn Street to Pall Mall, 1 furlong
8 poles in length. The Hay Market, a place for sale of
farm produce since Elizabeth's time, was removed to
Cumberland Market, Regent's Park, in 1831. The Arcade,
I think, was built when Her Majesty's Theatre was rebuilt
after having been burned down in 1867.

In an old directory for London OLD MARKET LANE,
Ratcliff, is given. Market Lane was a passage from Shadwell Market, S.E., to Lower Shadwell.

A Market Lane was off White Hart Street, Kennington
Lane, thirteen doors on the left from Kennington Cross.

There were two MILK LANES: one early one mentioned

M

in an indenture dated 3 April 1694 regarding property bequeathed by Sir William Pulteney—

to extend in length against the said street (called Old Sohoe alias Wardour Street) from an Alley or Passage called Milk Lane over against the end of Pulteney Street on the south part to Acton Road on the north . . . to abut east upon a Parcel of Ground theretofore called COLEMAN-HEDGE-LANE, then built upon, being on the back part of a New Street called Dean Street.

Another Milk Lane mentioned in Cary's *Guide for Hackney Coach Fares* (1801) was off Farmer Street, Upper Shadwell, and was 30 poles in length.

Leaving Shadwell going westwards, past New and Old Gravel Lanes, already described, were three lanes—ARTICHOKE LANE (demolished), RED MAID LANE (in 1772 map—now Redmead) and GREAT HERMITAGE LANE, now Street. The latter was named after a Hermitage on the site (in which dwelt a Hermit). This afterwards became a Brewery.

In Harrison's England we find: 'A great blow by gunpowder houses in a place called BOOLYES LANE neere the Armitage in Wapping on Tuesday the 3rd day of July 1657. In which were 250 barrels of gunpowder consumed.' I have not been able to trace this lane.

Another Artichoke Lane was at the south end of Virginia Street, about 150 yards northward from Wapping Street. Yet another at Newington Causeway, and, according to *New View of London*, 1708, on the south side of Cannon Street near Laurence Pountney Hill. It is shown in Noorthouck's map of Candlewick and Langbourne Wards between Green Lettuce Lane and St. Laurence Pountney Lane. ARTICHOKE HEAD LANE was near the Hermitage.

CHAPTER VIII

THEN WE COME TO NIGHTINGALE LANE WHICH separates St. Katharine's Docks from London Docks, and derives its name from the men of the Cnihten (Knight's) Guild: it was originally called CNIHTEN GUILD LANE. King Edgar granted to a company of thirteen Knights a piece of land hereabouts with liberty to form a guild on condition that each of them should victoriously accomplish three combats: one above the ground, one under the ground, and the third in the water. 'All of which was gloriously performed, and the same day the King named it Knighten Guild', says Stow.

This guild was held by the heirs of the thirteen Knights until the reign of Henry I, when they took upon themselves the brotherhood and the benefits of the newly established Priory of the Holy Trinity within Aldgate, assigned their 'soke' (Port-soken, without the port or gate), and offered upon the altars of the Church the several charters of their guild.

In the seventeenth century this was a real country lane. On 24 July 1629, Charles I hunted a stag from Wanstead and killed in a garden in this lane, 'much to the detriment of the tenant's herbs'.

It is now a street carrying such heavy traffic that on the 12th of November 1925 the roadway caved in to a

163

depth of some 12 feet about 100 yards from the Upper East Smithfield end.

There was a place in the lane called Frog Island which probably accounted for a jumpy feeling experienced late at night there.

In the General Sessions of Peace Rolls, 1 April forty-two Elizabeth, a man was proclaimed as having commenced building a playhouse in this lane, contrary to Her Majesty's Orders set down in Her Court of Starchamber. At the bottom of Nightingale Lane Burr Street runs westwards. Off this was a LITTLE NIGHTINGALE LANE. Dodsley gives another Nightingale Lane as being in Fore Street, Limehouse. Fore Street is described in Large's *Way about London* as the third on the right down Three Colt Street. That would be the east end of the present-named Narrow Street. A turning to the right in Commercial Road East at Britannia Bridge was Maize Row and the second turning on the left was Nightingale Lane.

In Nightingale Lane, from Clapham to Wandsworth, the Rev. C. H. Spurgeon resided.

A lane of this name is at Hornsey, Greenwich, Wanstead and Deptford.

In Noorthouck's map of 1772 ST. CATHARINE'S LANE is marked east of Little Tower Hill, and running south out of East Smithfield (now Upper East Smithfield) with a somewhat T-shaped bend at the end, one arm leading into Little Tower Hill.

In this map what was marked as Lower East Smithfield in Bacon's map of 1895 is shown as St. Catherine's: marked in P.O. map for 1918 St. Katherine's Way, off which is shown in Noorthouck's map a PILLORY LANE running northwards to the junction of Red Cross Street and Butcher Row. These three latter places were all wiped out in the formation of St. Catherine's Docks, which took their name, as did the lane, from the ancient Royal Hospital of St. Catherine, originally founded by Matilda, Queen of Stephen, in 1148, which with the ancient Collegiate Church attached to it occupied the site.

There was a Pillory Lane by Butcher Row, Fenchurch Street. This Row was probably at Aldgate at the end of Fenchurch Street. I have been unable to trace any other in the neighbourhood.

There is a Nightingale Lane at Balham, and there w as one near Kenwood, HAMPSTEAD LANE.

In my notes I find MIDDLE SHADWELL LANE at 50 East Smithfield, Virginia . . . Hill. Fifty, Upper East Smithfield (as it is called now) is opposite the entrance to West London Dock. I think the lane must have been wiped out when the goods line from Leman Street Station to West London Dock was made. Virginia Street is still there— on the opposite side of the road—the first on the right going east in St. George Street.

The name of the Hill I am unable to decipher—though I wrote it down myself! Nor can I remember whence I got the information. From the same unknown source I had MIDDLE TURNING LANE, Shadwell.

After many digressions without explanation let us return to the neighbourhood of Vintry Ward. KNIGHTRIDER LANE was the name given to the houses at the 'corner of Bredestrete upon Knightrider-lane in the Parish of St. Mildred' in 1349. This is now Queen Victoria Street, previously Old Fish Street, and Knightrider Street.

WRINGWREN LANE is described by Stow as being the west end of the church of St. Thomas Apostle, near the boundary of Vintry Ward, south of Turnbase Lane. Johanna Travers in her will dated 1295 left a big stone hall and a little stone hall and two cellars called 'Helle' with a wharf in FATTES LANE in the parish of St. James Vintry to be sold.

A house called Little Helle (parvum Helle) occurs in a deed enrolled in 1343, Roll 70 (130). Among the archives of St. Paul's Cathedral is a certificate of an admission to a Chantrey 'commonly called Helle'.

KERION LANE (as spelled and described by Stow) was in Royall Street, 'so called from one Kerion some time dwelling there', and contained 'divers fair houses for merchants and the Glazier's Hall. At the south corner of Royall Street is the fair parish church of St. Martin Vintry' (destroyed in the Great Fire). KIRONELANE in a will dated 1295 is described as adjoining Soper Lane near the church of St. Michael, Paternoster Royal.

Richard Chaucer, vintner, step-grandfather to the poet, in his will dated 12 April 1349, bequeathed to the parishioners and parson of St. Mary de Aldermariechirche his entire tenement with tavern in the street called 'La Riole' at the corner of KYROUNLANE. The greater part of the street was demolished in the formation of Cannon Street. King Stephen had his residence in it, at Tower Royal, as also had the Duke of Norfolk in the reign of Richard III.

CRESSYNGHAM LANE is described in a will dated 1441 as being in 'the parish of St. James, Garlikhithe, to the north of a tenement in the parishes of this and St. Martin Vintry' of which the east boundary was STODIE'S LANE, described by Stow as included in the gift by Sir John Stodie to the Vintners' Company of the site on which Vintners' Hall afterwards stood.

If Cressyngham Lane were to the west of the site it would be identical with the now Anchor Alley—then Lane—at 68 Upper Thames Street. Stow says it was previously called SPITTLE LANE. John Cressyngham was one of those retained to advise Mayors touching affairs of the City for Vintry Ward in 1347. Anchor Alley was called PALMER'S LANE in 1439–48. Plumbers' Hall was there.

An Anchor Lane, Mile End Road, is given in the Post Office List for 1857.

WESTON and WOLSEY LANES were adjacent to the Coldharbour, a thirteenth-century mansion in Thames Street and in which the Black Prince is said to have resided in 1370, before Alice Ferrars—the mistress of Edward III—owned it. She is said to have built many houses adjacent to the great gate of the inn between Weston and Wolsey Lanes.

In 1311 William de Caxstone, buriller, left his tenement in WOLSISLANE to be sold to pay his debts and to fulfil his testament, Robert Persone, skinner, being preferred as purchaser.

COLDHARBOUR LANE led south out of Upper Thames Street a little to the east of the present Suffolk Lane. Another Coldharbour Lane, a very long, winding street, runs from Denmark Hill to Brixton Oval.

CAMPION LANE was south out of Upper Thames Street to the river by Hay Wharf Lane. The site is now occupied by the City of London Brewery and entrance. It was mentioned as del Hay Wharf in a deed of date 1235.

WYVENELANE was in the parish of S. Mary Somersete (then in Upper Thames Street) according to the will, dated 21 December 1355, of John de Gloucestre, fishmonger.

COMMON LANE (the Common Staires in Queen Elizabeth's time) was the previous name of Sand Wharf, thus called by Horwood in 1799. Now Wheatsheaf Wharf at 1 Upper Thames Street, east of Puddle Dock. Appears to have been renamed about 1848–51.

The only reference I have been able to find to CONDIT LANE, Dowgate, is the name on a tradesman's token issued to a house in this lane, dated 1649–72, name Dan Burry, woodmonger. No. 363 in the Guildhall.

CATTENE LANE is mentioned as being in the Ward of Wolmar de Essex, which has been identified with Billingsgate Ward in the Hundred Rolls of the third of Edward I.

ST. MARY HILL LANE (now St. Mary-at-Hill) was so called because the parish church of St. Mary is on the ascent from Billingsgate to Eastcheap. The church was rebuilt by Wren after the Great Fire.

To this church, annually, on the next Sunday after Midsummer, the Fellowship of the Porters of London came in the morning. Whilst psalms were being read they went two by two to the Communion table rails and placed their offerings in two basins set there. The inhabitants of the parish, and their wives, followed, did likewise, and the money was afterwards given to poor decrepit porters of the Company. The rector from 1789 till 1806 (buried in the Chancel) was Brand, compiler of *Popular Antiquities*, and also Secretary to the Society of Antiquaries.

In 1529 Sir William Butter, Mayor in 1507, left his house Le Baskett to the Grocers' Company. In 1536 it was described as being in the occupation of the Drapers' Company, being to the east of a tenement called le Sonne which fronted on St. Mary Hill Lane.

Tenements and wharves in 'WIREHALLE LANE in the parish of St. Mary-at-Hill' are mentioned in a will of 1477–78.

Dodsley gives a 'WORCESTER PLACE LANE in Thames Street'.

ROOD LANE runs from 41 Eastcheap to 23 Fenchurch Street.

So called of a roode there placed in the Churchyard of St. Margaret Pattens, whilst the old church was taken down and again newly built, during which time the oblations made to the rood were employed towards the building of the church; but in the year 1538, about 23rd May, in the morning, the said rood was found to have been, on the night preceding, by people unknown, broken all to pieces, together with the Tabernacle wherein it had been placed,

says Stow. This lane was previously called PATTEN'S LANE because pattens were, at one time, usually sold and made in the lane. The church, mentioned as early as 1344, was in Whittington's gift, and was again rebuilt after the Great Fire.

Harben says BRETASK LANE may be identical with Dyers' Hall Wharf at 95 Upper Thames Street. In the third of Henry VIII the Dyers' Company claimed this lane, but the claim was disallowed; it was found to be a common lane of the city, named after the house la Bretaske and wharf adjoining here, owned in 1343 by Thomas de Porkeslee who had had the lane closed up some time previously. The house was an embattled house erected in 1338 near the Tower in what was called Galley Row or, more commonly, Petty Wales. It cost £126 and was partly built of Caen stone with the hall of timber boards nailed with ship's nails, evidently built (says Stow) by shipwrights, and not house carpenters, and seemed, as it were, a galley—the keel turned upwards. The building had fallen to ruin and been let out for stabling of horses 'to tipplers of beer and such like, amongst others Mother Mampudding (as they termed her)', who for many years kept the greater part of the house for victualling.

Stow doubted its antiquity 'since there were no worm nor rottenness apparent', concluding (in the first edition) with 'but I leave every man to his own judgment, and pass to other matters'.

SOUTHAM LANE TEMESTREET is mentioned in a letter book dated 1383 with respect to a case of felony. I have not been able to trace it.

MINCING LANE, from Fenchurch Street to Tower Street, City, is the great market for tea, sugar, spices, and colonial products generally. Stow explains that it derives its name from tenements there sometime pertaining to the Minchuns or Nuns of St. Helen's in Bishopsgate Street.

In a will dated 1312 it is spelled MENIONELANE, and in another of the same year MANGONELANE. Previous to this, in 1291, in the will of Henry de Lewes, MANIMANELANE, in the will of Roger Vothot, same year, MONECHENILANE.

In 1349 a Brewery in MYNIOUNLANE was willed to William, kinsman of Henry Wymond, woolmonger.

The Abbot of Colchester's Inn was in this lane. Mention is made of payments to be made at it in 1390 and in 1461. Colchester Abbey had, at the time of the Dissolution, an inn here called 'le Bell' valued at £5 6s. 8d. with a garden valued at £1 6s. 8d.

This lane was, of old times, much frequented by men from Genoa and those parts, called Galley men because they came in the galleys which brought wine and merchandise to Galley Key east of the Customs House. These had a small coin called Galley Halfpennies which were forbidden in Henry IV's time and by Parliament in 1417, which enacted that any person bringing into this realm halfpence, suskinges, or dodkins (Bailey gives the latter as worth about a farthing) should be punished as a thief, and he that taketh or payeth shall leese a hundred shillings, whereof the King was to have half and he that would sue the other half. Stow says he, in his youth, had seen them passed current 'with some difficulty'.

Dickens (in *Our Mutual Friend*) has Bella Wilfer sit waiting in the canary-coloured chariot at the corner of Mincing Lane and Fenchurch Street while her father asks for leave to dine with her at Greenwich.

Sir John Robinson, Lieutenant of the Tower, lived here. The Clothworkers' Hall is at No. 41.

In the inquest dated 16 July 1338 on the death of Sir Giles de Badlesmere it was mentioned that he had, besides other property within Aldgate, a tenement and garden in LIME STREET LANE.

The continuation of Barbican eastwards is now Beech Street, off which runs BEECH LANE to 51 Whitecross Street. Beech Lane was the old name of Beech Street referred to by Stow as stretching from Red Cross Street to White Cross Street, as having been, peradventure, named after Nicholas de la Beech, Lieutenant of the

Tower of London, deposed in the thirteenth of Edward III. It then had beautiful houses of stone, brick and timber. One great house was Drewry House belonging to Sir Drewe Drewrie, formerly the lodging of the Abbot of Ramsey. After being occupied by Mr. Keene, a currier, Prince Rupert lived in it. Part of it was, in 1792, made use of by Dissenters as a place of worship.

In 1540 Lady Irene Askew made a gift of eight almshouses of brick and timber to be built in the lane, rent free, for eight poor widows of the Drapers' Company, of which her husband had been a member—also Mayor in 1533.

In GOLDEN, GOLDING, or GOLDYNG LANE at the end of Beech Street, Richard Gallard, of Islington, Esquire, founded thirteen almshouses, rent free. From a survey of the Manor of Finsbury in 1567 printed by Strype, the lane then had good gardens and tenements, inns, and a brewery. Early in the next century the Fortune Theatre was built there by Mr. Alleyn, the comedian, and founder of Dulwich College, on the site of the building which was originally the nursery for the children of Henry VIII. Alleyn purchased the lease of this from one Brest for £120.

At 54 Curtain Road, Shoreditch, is HOLYWELL LANE, named from a holy well once there, and a house of Benedictine nuns of that name, founded by a Bishop of London and rebuilt with the church of St. John and the chapel by Sir Thomas Lovell of Lincoln's Inn, Treasurer to the Household of Henry VII.

Near St. Leonard's Church, says Stow, 'are builded two publique houses for the acting and shewe of comedies, trajedies, and histories, for recreation'. One was called the Courtain, the other the Theatre, both standing on the south-west in the field.

This gave the name to The Curtain Theatre, built in Holywell Lane and Curtain Road.

CHAPTER IX

HERE FOLLOW A NUMBER OF LANES (WITH WHAT particulars I have been able to glean) in some attempt at alphabetical order; the only order —with interpolations—I can suggest; otherwise chaos.

ABBEY LANE, Kilburn, at 250 Belsize Road, is probably a reminiscence of Bluff King Hal's days when Kilburn was a small rural village nestling round a priory. Here are still some old country cottages; their front gardens being now wood-yards and scrap-iron heaps. It runs into West-end Lane, out of which at No. 341 runs Mill Lane to Shootup Hill.

There is a THREE MILL LANE at St. Leonard's Street, Poplar.

The Abbey Lane at Stratford recalls the Abbey founded there by the Cistercian monks in 1135.

Of ABBEY MILLS LANE, near the Mills Pumping Station there, the same remark applies.

A tenement in 'ADBRIGHT LANE in the parish of Aldermanbury being the eighteenth of twenty counting from the Church of Aldermanbury' is an extract from the Harleian MSS. 36 Henry VIII.

'ADDELANE in the parish of St. Alban de Wodestrete' is mentioned in the will of John de Norhampton (tailor) in 1305, who bequeathed a tenement there. Might have been either Addle Street or Lad Lane, both being in the vicinity.

ATHELANE was an early name for Addle Street in the parish of St. Alban's de Wodestrete, in the reign of Edward III, also in 1560.

'Addelane, parish of St. Gregory, London, near the tenement of the Abbot of Petresburgh', is mentioned in William de Pertenhale's will of 1348. St. Gregory stood in St. Paul's Churchyard, about where now is Queen Anne's statue, so this lane would not be the same as the first-mentioned Addelane.

ALDEN'S LANE I have a mention of, but no real trace can I find. Probably Old Dean's Lane. Off Addle Street is PHILIP LANE. On the west side of this was an ancient inn, a replica of the sign of which—an ape sitting on its haunches eating an apple, with the initials $\frac{B}{M}$ and date 1670—is built into the wall of a house here. A modern sculpture of a cock, a little further east, preserves the memory of the old Cock Inn at Cock Court.

Another Philip Lane runs from Tottenham Cross to West Green.

ALL FARTHING LANE runs from Wandsworth Common to GARRATT LANE—POUND LANE is at Willesden and POVERTY LANE is marked in Rocque's map of 1747 as off Brook Street, Grosvenor Square. ALL HALLOWS LANE probably adjoined the church of that name in Upper Thames Street, the west side of which was removed in 1865 for the building of Cannon Street Station.

ALMNES LANE. A house in the parish of St. Leonard,

Eastcheap, in this-named lane was demised to his wife Cristina by Reginald de Canefeld in 1322.

ALWYNE LANE is at 94 Canonbury Road and reminds us of Henry Fitz Alwyn, the first Mayor of London, who was Mayor of the city for twenty-four years.

ARONNES LANE. In the *Calendar of Wills in the Court of Husting* dated 1449 tenements are mentioned within the parish of St. Peter-the-Less in Themestrete situate between the lane called FRESSHFISHLANE and the lane called KYNGESLANE, otherwise Aronnes Lane.

ARUNDEL LANE is named in 1422 with reference to a tenement at the corner of it in the parish of All-Hallows-upon-the-Solar (i.e. the Less) in Themestrete.

AUGUR'S LANE, Plaistow, is mentioned in the Post Office *List of Streets*, etc., for 1920.

AXE LANE was probably Axe Yard on the left side of Grub Street (now Milton Street). The lane is mentioned in Forster's *Life of Oliver Goldsmith* in an anecdote told by the poet, about 1769, starting, 'When I lived among the beggars in Axe Lane'.

There are a few old cottages in ANGLER'S LANE at 227 Kentish Town Road.

ATWOOD LANE, in Rocque's 1763 map, then ran from Cromwell Road, Kensington, to Old Brompton Road, where it came out opposite THISTLE GROVE LANE. It is now called Ashburn Place and ends at Wetherby Place.

SALLAD LANE was from Old Brompton Road (to the east of Thistle Grove Lane) to Fulham Road, where it came out opposite what was then called (in 1840 map) Bolton Park Place, but is now incorporated in Church Street. Sallad Lane has become Selwood Terrace.

Thistle Grove Lane covers part of the site of what was known over a century ago as Brompton Heath. The author of the *Peerage and Commoners of England*—John Burke—lived here.

West of Thistle Grove Lane in Fulham Road is Gunter Grove, which runs to King's Road, Chelsea. In Large's *Way About London*, POOLES LANE is given as being the first on the left in King's Road west of Gunter Grove. That is now Uverdale Road.

BAGNIO LANE was in Newgate Street where the Bagnio was built by Turkish merchants and opened in 1679, for sweating, hot bathing and cupping. It was renamed Bath Street in 1843, but was originally PINCOCK or PENTECOST-LANE and contained slaughter-houses for the butchers, between St. Nicholas' Shambles and Butcher Alley, near Stinking Lane already described.

ST. NICHOLAS SHAMBLES LANE is mentioned in *Ancient Deeds* as 'leading from St. Nicholas de Westmacekaria to the City Wall'.

BAGLEY'S LANE is at 41 New King's Road, Fulham.

A BALAAM'S LANE is at Southgate.

In Nicholson's *New View of London*, 1708, BANISTER'S LANE is described as being 'on the east side of Blackfriars, a passage to Charles Street (nigh the Thames) near the middle'.

A BANNISTER LANE is marked, in an 1840 map, running from Wells Street, Hackney, to the back of St. Thomas's Schools, nearly opposite London Lane.

BARE LANE was off Gravel Lane.

In a will dated 1285 Master William de Wlchirchehaw bequeathed shops situate in 'BAREMANE LANE in the parish of St. Mary Wooheoth or St. Mary de Newchirche'.

N

A BARLEYMOW LANE was at Chiswick.

BARNSBURY LANE ran from Upper Street, Islington, to Liverpool Road. With Albany Street, from Liverpool Road to Thornhill Road, it now forms Barnsbury Road.

BARTON LANE is mentioned by Stow as being (in 1722) out of Tower Street. Have not been able to trace it.

BATTESLANE, otherwise HAYWHARFLANE, is mentioned in the will of James Fynche, 1508. A couple of hundred years previously William de Combe left to his daughter Isabella intail the reversion of a cellar and solar in the parish of All-Hallows-at-the-Hay in Haywharflane. This lane was at the North end of All-Hallows-the-More in Thames Street. Stow says 'now lately a great brewhouse built by Henry Campion, Esquire'. Then there was one other lane, sometime called Woolfe's gate, in the ropery in the parish of All-Hallows-the-Less, of later time called WOLFES LANE, says Stow. He says, also, 'that it is now out of use; for the lower part thereof upon the banks of the Thames is built by the late Earl of Shrewsburie, and the other end is built on and stopped up by the Chamberlain of London'.

There is a WOLVES LANE at Palmer's Green.

BEAVOR LANE runs from 281 King Street, Hammersmith, to Upper Mall.

BEAVIS LANE is the old name for HENEAGE, INNAGE, or IMAGE LANE. It is so marked in Ogilby and Morgan's 1677 map. Stow says, HENNEAGE LANE, otherwise called LOUSIE or LOUSY LANE (it is so called in the *Review of London*, 1728). In 1732 it is referred to as 'LOUSE LANE by Creechurch Lane'. It runs from 16 Bevis Marks to Bury Street.

A large house belonging to the Bassets and afterwards

to the Abbots of Bury in Suffolk was called Buries Markes
—corruptly Bevis Markes. Since the dissolution of the
Abbey of Bury it belonged to Thomas Heneage, and to
Sir Thomas Heneage, his son. Hence the renaming.

Dodsley gives a SUGARBAKER'S LANE as being at Duke's
Place. Duke's Place is also mentioned in the Post Office
List for 1857, off Duke Street, Aldgate, and is so marked
in Moggs' map dated 1840.

In the Aldgate Ward map for 1772 the third turning
on the left from Aldgate in Shoemaker's Row (now Duke
Street) is named Mark Lane. This would refer to the house
mentioned—Buries Markes. I have not seen this shown
in any other map nor mentioned anywhere. This leads
into Broad Court, thence through Adam's Court to
Sugarbaker's Lane which ends at King Street. The last-
named lane appears to be Meter Street now.

There is a SUGAR HOUSE LANE at Stratford in which is
Messrs. Stewart's refinery.

St. Mary Axe is termed ST. MARY AXE LANE in Rocque's
1747 map.

CREECHURCH LANE, Aldgate, was the name given to the
lane where, on the north side of Leadenhall Street, is the
church of St. Katharine Cree, built on the site of the old
church taken down in 1628. The ceremonies connected
with the consecration of the newer church greatly added
to the feeling against Laud (when Bishop of London) who
conducted them. In the church is a pillar of the old
church retained to show that the level had to be raised
15 feet.

On 6 October the 'Lion Sermon' is preached here, for
which Sir John Gayer (Lord Mayor), in his will in 1648,

left £200 in memory of his deliverance from the jaws of a lion in Arabia.

A 'Flower Sermon' is also preached here—to children —on Whitsun-Tuesday, when every child presents a nose-gay. At the original sign of a Crown and Three Sugar Loaves in Creechurch Lane is what is claimed to be the oldest teaman's in the world.

Another shop sign, very rare, used to be in the lane— the Oatsheaf, as appears from a trader's token.

CREECHIN LANE is a corruption of Creechurch Lane.

Until 1894 the lane extended only so far north as Bury Street. In that year it was continued into St. James's Place and the former name of King Street disappeared. It was called, in the plans of Holy Trinity Priory, in 1592, 'The way oute of Allgat Streat into Creechurch monastery'.

BEGGAR'S LANE, according to Strype, was 'an open space into Charterhouse Yard and so into Smithfield where the beggars usually plied'.

BELBARBURES LANE is mentioned in a sixteenth-century document, in the Bodleian Library at Oxford, on the topography and divisions of the ancient borough of Stepney, as the place where 'Stratford Warde begennyth'. COLIER LANE is also mentioned.

BELL LANE runs out of Wentworth Street, Spitalfields The curiously named Frying Pan Alley is off this lane.

In Rocque's map of London, 1746, the road running from the top of Sloane Street to Brompton and Little Chelsea is called Bell Lane. In a later map the west end of the present Brompton Road, off which ran GORE LANE, was marked Brompton Lane. The next lane to Gore Lane

England's Lane. N.W.

westward was CROMWELL LANE. The Rev. A. G. L'Estrange in his *Village of Palaces* says the present Cromwell Road was called Cromwell Lane and that there was a conduit with a small square building for the water brought by pipes laid by Henry VIII from Kensington to the Palace at Chelsea, which existed there till the middle of the nineteenth century.

Bell Lane near Lisham (Lisson) Green is mentioned in *Pleasant Revels in Paddington*. This was probably the present Bell Street, off Edgware Road.

BELSIZE LANE is but a name-place lane, but in its serpentine twists from the bottom of Fitzjohn's Avenue to Haverstock Hill, and its rural look, in parts it is still a 'lane' proper.

While as far north-west as this I must mention ENGLAND'S LANE, off Haverstock Hill. Anything less like a lane than this! But I had presented to me very kindly—by Mr. Charles I. Strachan, who lives hard by—a photograph of it when it really was a most charming and delightful country lane. I treasure this. My sketch is from it.

Having mentioned a London Lane, England's Lane had to be referred to. I find that in Davies's *New Map of London* for 1854 it is called INGRAM'S LANE.

In the Post Office List for 1857 it is described as England's Lane, St. John's Park Road, Hampstead.

BILLITER LANE (now Street) runs from Leadenhall Street to Fenchurch Street opposite Mark Lane. Stow says the correct name was 'BELZETTAR, of the first builder and owner thereof, now corruptly called Billitar'.

Professor W. W. Skeat says it was called BELL-ZETER'S LANE, the lane where the bell-founders live.

Billiter Square, off No. 11 in the (now) street, marks the site of the old metal-workers' factories. A wealthy alderman, Walter le Poter, was of this trade, and presented all the brazen pots for the kitchen, infirmary, and other offices of the Grey Friars.

Strype describes it: 'Billiter Lane, a place consisting formerly of poor and ordinary houses, where it seems needy and beggarly people used to inhabit.' Whence the proverb used in ancient times, 'A Bawdy Beggar of Billiter Lane', which Sir Thomas Moore used in his book against Tyndal. It is very different now—a handsome avenue. An act was passed in 1760 to enlarge the passage of Billiter Lane to 30 feet by pulling down the houses on the east side.

In 1590, when three houses were being built between Belzetter's Lane and Lime Street (which before was a large garden plot enclosed with a brick wall), beneath the wall was found another wall, of stone, with an arched stone gate, and gates of timber to be closed to the street. The iron hinges remained on their staples on both sides. In the wall were square windows on both sides of the gate. Since Stow says he estimated this wall to be above two fathoms deep, it is to be seen how greatly the ground of the city has been raised. He said it seemed to be the ruins of a house buried in the fire which happened in King Stephen's reign. That which was the hall of a mansion of a Lord Mayor of London was, over five hundred years ago, a cellar under an inn with 18, 16, and 12 steps (each of about 7 inches deep).

A different spelling is found in a case in 1320, in which permission to prosecute an action as to forty shillings rent of a brewhouse in BELHETERESLANE was asked for by Laurencia de Sterteford, which she claimed to hold by feoffment of Gilbert de la Marche, her father, and not of the said Gilbert, her son.

BILLET LANE runs between Higham Hill and Chapel end.

BINGLE'S LANE is now Bingley Road, Victoria Docks.

BIRD'S LANE is mentioned in Lockie's *Topography*, 1816, as being at Stangate, Lambeth, the second on the left from Westminster Bridge. Stangate—where the old stairs were—has been wiped out by St. Thomas's Hospital and Lambeth Palace Road; but in Moggs' 1840 map the first on the left there is Stangate Street and the second Crozier Street, both of which are still there.

BISHOP'S LANE was off DAWES LANE, Fulham. Both are now promoted to Roads.

BLACK LANE, marked in Rocque's 1763 map, was a lane which ran from near the north of Battle Bridge, west of Copenhagen Fields, straight to the west end of Hornsey Lane. The whole length of the present York Road, Brecknock Road, and Dartmouth Park Hill exactly coincide with it.

BLACK BOY LANE is described in Lockie's *Topography*, 1816, as being at Poplar, half a mile on the left from Commercial Road opposite the Harrow.

Another lane of the same name is at West Green, Tottenham. The lane next to the first-mentioned Black Boy Lane, in Rocque's 1763 map, is named BLACKWELL LANE.

BLACK HORSE LANE is off FERRY LANE, Tottenham.

BLACK LION LANE runs from King Street, Hammersmith, to Chiswick Mall (which part is now called Hammersmith Terrace).

BLADEN LANE ran between The Grove and Cottingham Road, Earl's Court. It is now called Bolton Gardens.

BLACKLANDS LANE was off Symon's Street, Sloane Square. It was just at Blacklands Lane in the early part of the eighteenth century, on the old common, that an enterprising individual set up a turnpike and took tolls until the Chelsea authorities intervened—to his financial disgust. In 1810 Blacklands was in King's Road opposite Whitelands, at the back of Colvell's Nursery—the second coach turning on the right from Sloane Square towards Fulham and Blackland's Lane was the continuation of it to Brompton by the Marlborough Tavern. Blacklands Terrace is there now. The lane seems to have been on the site of the late Marlborough Road, which, with Keppel Street, has evidently been rebuilt and turned into Sloane and Draycott Avenues. Elystan Street appears to have taken the place of Old College Street, and Marlborough Square—just off the last named—to have disappeared and only a short street remains.

There was a WHITELANDS LANE near the house of that name.

The mansion of Blacklands was afterwards a school. In Cary's *New Guide* for ascertaining coach fares, etc., dated 1801, in 'places passed through from Sloane Square to Chelsea College, the first turning—one furlong, ten poles from Sloane Square—is the road leading to Blackland's School'. Then HANGMAN'S LANE or the 'road to Chelsea College' follows. Why this lane was called Hangman's I do not know. But there was a lane at East Wapping which was named Hangman's Lane for good and sufficient reason. From the time of Henry VI pirates had been hanged there. In a chronicle of London during this reign is the information that two bargemen were hanged for murdering three Flemings and a child—'and there they hanged till the water had washed them by ebbing and flowing'. As late as 1735 Williams the pirate was hanged at Execution Dock, and afterwards, in chains, at Bugsby's Hole, near Blackwall. In *Londinopolis* by Howill, 1657, we read that 'from the Liberties of St. Katharine's to Wapping 'tis yet in the memory of man there never was a house standing but the gallowes'.

A curious misnomer occurred in the precincts of the Tower. The style of a place where poor refugees from 'Hammes and Guynes' were permitted to live by Queen Mary after our loss of Calais, was corrupted into 'Hangman's Gains'.

BLYTHE LANE, now road, runs from Hammersmith to Shepherd's Bush Road. It scarcely suggests happiness, in parts.

BOLISH LANE appears in the will of Wm. Haunsard, 1349, who left a brewhouse in this lane, in the parish of Holy Trinity, to his daughter Johanna. This must have been the brewhouse mentioned in Noorthouck's *History*, with other buildings belonging to King Edward III's Victualling Office, which stood upon the site of the New Abbey (called also the Abbey of Grace, and Eastminster) built upon the pest-ground, and named the churchyard of the Holy Trinity.

BONNER'S LANE—part of which is now Bonner's Street —is off Green Street, Bethnal Green. Here was Bishop

Bonner's Hall, a little to the west of the site of which now stands the Hospital of the National Children's Home and Orphanage, the gardens of which are the remains of an avenue formerly extending from Old Ford Lane to the principal entrance of the Hall, which is traditionally said to have been the residence of the Bishop. In an 1829 map the lane is a curly one extending from Green Street across Old Ford Road to the Regent's Canal. It has evidently been partly wiped out in the making of St. James's and Approach roads. The Hall Farm, a curious structure of plaster and brickwork, stood, until about 1850, near what is now the western entrance to Victoria Park. The neighbourhood before the Park was formed was known as Botany Bay—from so many of its inhabitants being sent to the real one.

BOOKBINDER LANE is mentioned in a Harleian MS. as being in London in 1593–4.

In the thirteenth century Chertsey Abbey had a Court in London near Fishwharf in the parish of St. Mary Somerset on the west side of BOSSE LANE. Stow mentions a Bosse Alley as being in Billingsgate Ward on the north side, east of Trig Lane, 'so called of a boss of spring water continually running, which standeth by Billingsgate against this alley, and was sometime made by The Executors of Richard Whittington'.

BOUNDARY LANE is at 71 Camberwell Road and extends to Providence Street, Walworth. In it are L.C.C. Schools. Five BOWLING GREEN LANES are mentioned here. One still remains at 66 Farringdon Road; in which, in 1668, were two noted greens for this pastime, spoken of with much contempt by honest old Stow. He complained that by the means of closing in the common grounds, our archers, for want of room to shoot abroad, crept into bowling alleys, and ordinary dicing houses, nearer home, where they found room enough to hazard their money at unlawful games; at which, he says, 'he left them to take their pleasure'.

A second Bowling Green Lane is off Newcomen Street, Borough; a third—'lane' being changed to 'walk'—in the third turning on the right in Pitfield Street, Hoxton.

Another was at 27 High Street, Marylebone, between Paddington and Paradise Streets; while the fifth Bowling-Green Lane, marked in Mogg's 1840 map and named in Lockie's 1810 list, was the first turning on the right in the then New Road (Marylebone Road) next to the 'Yorkshire Stingo'. It is now part of Seymour Place. It was also called STINGO LANE, and named as such in the *London Post Office Directory for* 1866. From here Shillibeer's first London omnibuses started in 1829. In the Metropolitan Board of Works Expenses Estimate for year ending March 1871, the sum of £50,000 appears for the Stingo Lane improvements.

BOWYER LANE is now Wyndham Road, from Camberwell New Road to Camberwell Road, and the old WINDMILL LANE near it is now Avenue Road. Here was the old Camberwell, otherwise Freeman's Mill. As early as 1307 a capital messuage and a windmill in Camberwell are mentioned, the former rated at 6s. 8d., the latter at 10s. per annum. The Bowyer family, responsible for the name of the first-mentioned lane, settled in Camberwell in the time of Henry VIII. The family mansion—the manor-house of Camberwell—Buckingham, near The Green, was built in Queen Elizabeth's time. It is said that Sir Christopher Wren stayed here during the rebuilding of St. Paul's Cathedral, and that James II hid himself here some time previous to his escape. It was bought by the London, Chatham and Dover Railway Company, and pulled down in 1861.

Bowyer Lane had some undesirable inhabitants. Greenacre the murderer lived there in 1836. A family living in the lane exhibited in their house, at a shilling a head, the executed body of one of their own relations who had been stealing horses.

Robert Son or Soun, fishmonger, left, in 1321, a house in 'BRANDREESLANE, in the parish of St. Botolph', to his son Thomas.

BROAD BRIDGES LANE is given in an old directory list as being at Shadwell.

A BRIDGE LANE is mentioned in the same list as being in Brewer Street. This, I expect, is BRIDLE LANE from Brewer Street to Beak Street, Golden Square.

BROOMHOUSE LANE (now Road) is at Fulham, from Hurlingham Road to Broomhouse Dock. The Hurlingham Club is in it and DAISY LANE runs off it.

BROWN LANE is off Canonbury Square.

Brown's Lane, Red Lion Street, Spitalfields, is now Hanbury Street, next to Trueman, Hanbury & Buxton's Brewery. Barber's Alley is in this Lane.

BUNHILL LANE ran by the side of the fields of that name.

BROOK'S LANE is off Vine Street, Tooley Street.

BROOK'S WHARF LANE at 48 Upper Thames Street: Strype mentions it in 1755.

BURTON LANE is off Highgate Hill.

BURTON HOLE LANE (and Farm) at Mill Hill.

CABBAGE LANE, in a *New View of London*, 1708, is given as being in James Street, Westminster. It is now called Castle Street. There was another of the same name in Long Lane.

In Roberts' *New Review of London*, 1728, he mentions a Powdered Beef Court in CABBAGE LANE, Westminster. Dodsley, in 1761, says Petty France was called Cabbage Lane. The then James Street is now Buckingham Gate. CASTLE LANE turns off it (with its lane resuscitated) and Petty France (now York Street) might easily have been part of a winding Cabbage Lane—the stalk of the cabbage. I have not been able to trace the one in Long Lane, nor in which Long Lane it was.

CANONBURY LANE is off Canonbury Square. No. 3 in this lane was the house from which, in 1818, a man named Rennett stole and took off to the Continent a boy of $3\frac{1}{2}$ years of age, the son of Mr. Horsley, a shipbroker, and his wife, the daughter of Charles Dignum, a popular singer. Rennett was caught and sentenced at the Old Bailey to seven years' transportation.

Opposite Canonbury Lane was KETTLE LANE, now Park Street. It is mentioned in the rolls of Canonbury Manor that H. Kettle had a house here in the second of Charles II, after whom the lane was named. There is a token extant of Joan Kettle at the sign of the Three Globes in Islington, 1667.

Of Castle Lanes, including the one just mentioned, there appear to have been six—the second one in Long Acre; a third, now Castle Street, ran out of SURREY LANE, Battersea Bridge Road. At the end of this Castle Lane, across the High Street, was a GREEN LANE.

HYDE LANE is at 118 Battersea Bridge Road. A little further on was a footpath to Surrey Lane, out of which at No. 13 ran SURREY LANE SOUTH. FOLLY LANE was also off Battersea Bridge Road.

A fourth Castle Lane was in Palace Street, Westminster; a fifth at Redcross Street, Deadman's Place, Southwark. That one is now also called Street.

The sixth Castle Lane, so called in 1353, was west of Puddle Wharf, between Blackfriars and the Thames. One great messuage here was the London lodging of the Prior of Okeborne in Wiltshire. Being of the French order, Henry V supplied this. According to records there was a mill (or mills) belonging to the Templars of the New Temple. King John in the first year of his reign granted a place in the Fleet, near Baynard's Castle, to make a mill, and the whole course of the waters of the Fleet to serve the mill.

CARKER'S LANE is at 51 Highgate Road. Out of the same road is also a COLLEGE LANE between Lady Somerset and Burghley Roads. Another College Lane is the fourth turning on the right in High Street, Homerton. College Lane was the old name for College Street, City.

CARLISLE LANE was in Mount Street, Lambeth, three doors south of the Marshgate, in an 1816 list. Now promoted to Street. Named after Carlisle House, which stood here from the thirteenth to sixteenth century, it was originally the Palace of the Bishops of Rochester, called then La Place. When it became the property of the Bishopric of Carlisle its name was changed. The Hedger's Almshouses, Holy Trinity Church, and the entrance to the Archbishop's Park are in this lane.

In a Harleian MS. of 1274 mention is made of two houses in the parish of St. George in the lane called CATE LANE. CECELIE'S LANE east of Warwick Lane in the parish of St. Faith, occupied now by Rose Street at 20 Newgate Street to Paternoster Square, is identical with DICER'S LANE, tenements in which are mentioned in many deeds of Henry III's time among the St. Paul's MSS. as being bounded by 'Venella Veteri's Decain', otherwise Eldeneslane, west, and by Cecelie's Lane de la Tur east.

Dicer's Lane is spelled DEZARSLANE in Hugh de Marny's will, 1334. In a document dated 1423, catalogued by Mr. Maxwell Lyte in the appendix to the ninth report of the Historical Manuscripts, it is called Dicer's Lane. It is otherwise called le Redye there.

I have a mention of a DICE KEY LANE. In Noorthouck's 1772 map the next key east of Billingsgate Dock is Smart's Key, next east to which is Great Dice Key. Then Little Dice Key, and next to that Temple Key. The lane must have been the entrance to one of the Dice Keys (Quays).

CATHERINE WHEEL LANE was behind the Thatched House Tavern in St. James's Street. Mary Granville, Mrs. Delany (the good old widow), lived here after the doctor's demise. The Little Thatched House was there in 1771.

CHARLES LANE is off High Street, St. John's Wood.

CHERRY GARDEN LANE leading to the Pier of that name, Rotherhithe.

Stow described CLARKE'S WELL LANE as being near unto so much of the church which remaineth to serve as a parish church of St. John, when he mentioned, besides Clarke's Well, 'Skinner Well, Fagge's Well, Jode Well, Loder's Well, Rede Well, etc., now dammed up'.

CLIFFORD'S INN LANE is now the Passage of that name leading to the Inn, in the Hall of which, after the Great Fire, sat Sir Matthew Hale and seventeen other judges to adjudicate upon the claims of the owners and tenants of burned houses. Forty thick folio volumes of decisions now in the British Museum give some idea of their task.

CLOAK LANE, from Dowgate Hill to Queen Street, was originally called Horse Bridge Street, because, Stow says, 'of such a bridge sometimes over the brook there, now vaulted over'. Elmes suggests its derivation from Cloaca, a sewer, which 'anciently ran along it from Queen Street into the Wallbrook'. Wheatly remarks that as its early name was HORSE BRIDGE LANE it is not likely in later times to have been called Cloak Lane from an *ancient* sewer.

The church of St. John Baptist was situate on Dowgate Hill, at the corner of Cloak Lane, afterwards a burying ground, and the church of St. Thomas the Apostle stood in the street or highway near this burying ground. Cutler's Hall was in this lane before removal to Warwick Lane.

COATS LANE—so marked in a 1772 map—is named Jew's Walk in a map dated 1840; now Old Ford Road. Cambridge Road, whence it started, was then called Dog Row.

COLD BATH LANE was in Church Street, Hackney. This street is now merged into Mare Street. According to Large's *Way about London* the lane was in Church Street, the second turning on the left past the railway bridge. Church Street commenced at London Lane in the old maps; but later Morning Lane was accounted the dividing line between Church and Mare Streets. I fancy Kenmure Road (that being now the second turning referred to) must be the site of the old lane. It originally led down to the Hackney Brook.

COLD BLOW LANE is mentioned in Morgan's *London Street Directory* (no date, but appears to be about 1881) as being in Old Kent Road. There is now a Cold Blow Lane, a continuation of Brocklehurst Street at Deptford; this street continues south as Brocklehurst Road, at the bottom of which is HART LANE. These two Cold Blow Lanes may be the same.

COLEHILL LANE runs from Fulham Palace Road to Munster Road.

CONEYHOPE LANE, Poultry, was the old name for Grocer's Hall Court. In Strype's 1720 map it is marked Grocer's Court. Matilda de Myms, in her will of April 1349, ordered her brewery near the chapel in CONYNG-HOPLANE to be sold.

So called of a sign of three conies hanging over a poulterer's stall at the end of the lane, which at one time was full of sponging-houses to which the Serjeants belonging to the Poultry Compter brought their prisoners and locked them up till they could make arrangements with their creditors; not to run them into prison.

CONEY HALL LANE is now Rolt Street, Evelyn Street, Deptford, nearly opposite old Grove Lane (now Street).

CONVENT LANE was at Brook Green, Hammersmith.

COOLY'S LANE described as at Brook Street, Ratcliffe. Brook Street runs from Devonport Street to Whitehorse Street. I cannot trace any lane named Cooly's, but there is a SCHOOLHOUSE LANE there. Possibly a corruption of that?

COOPER'S ARMS LANE was off High Street, Putney.

CROSSFIELD LANE runs from High Street to Church

Street, Deptford, coming into Church Street a little below COPPERAS LANE on the opposite side of the street. SLAUGHTER HOUSE LANE was a little further south and ran from Church Street to Creek Street. It is now all Creek Street, Deptford.

CORPORATION LANE from opposite the end of Bowling Green Lane to St. John Street, Clerkenwell, now Corporation Row.

COTTAGE LANE runs from 300 City Road to New Charles Street.

CREMORNE LANE was between, and parallel with, Dartrey Road and Seaton Street, running from the top of Blantyre Street, meeting Cremorne Road at the west end of Cheyne Walk. The Chapel appears to be built on the site of it.

COX'S LANE is at Shadwell, near which is old CUT-THROAT LANE. This—from Cock Hill to Brook Street—is now called Love Lane. What a change! From the tragic to the sublime! Might not this and other similarly named lanes have been named Cut Through? There is, or was, a few years ago, one actually so called and so marked in Bacon's map, running from Kingston Road to Putney Heath.

Another Cutthroat Lane was off Kingsland Road. Yet another at Islington. The present Barnsbury Street, running from Upper Street to Thornhill Road, rejoiced in the name of Cutthroat Lane when it was just a narrow passage leading from Upper Street to the Workhouse, until in 1791 the way was widened and houses were erected on the north side.

Another Cutthroat Lane (now Oldfield Road) ran from

47 Broughton Road, Stoke Newington, to Painsthorpe Road. Part of the garden wall of Defoe's house was in this Cutthroat Lane. Defoe's Road is close by. Here lived Daniel, who went to a boys' school on Stoke Newington Green and had, there, for schoolfellows, Samuel Wesley —father of John and Charles—and a boy named Crusoe!

CRAB LANE is mentioned as 'near Colliers Row, Shoreditch'.

The old CRAB TREE LANE, in a 1772 map, off Hackney Road, nearly opposite Union Road, is now Columbia Road. In Mogg's 1840 map it is called Crab Tree Row.

Another Crabtree Lane is off Fulham Palace Road to Woodland Road.

Old ELMS LANE, Craven Hill, Paddington, is now Craven Terrace, a continuation of Devonshire Terrace, and old CRAVEN LANE was the Park end of Leinster Terrace. Both lanes now form Leinster Gardens. These are marked in a Davies' 1854 map of London but not in an 1829 map, which latter gives the New Bagnigge Wells as being a few yards east of Elms Lane (nearly opposite the end of the Serpentine in Kensington Gardens) at the top of which ran Conduit Street, west and east (now Craven Road), a continuation of Praed Street off which still runs Spring Street.

In the *London Street Directory for* 1881 a CROWN LANE, St. Dunstan's Hill, is mentioned.

Dodsley mentions a DANCING LANE, Southwark, with a Priest's Yard coming out of it.

DEPTFORD LANE is given in the Post Office List for 1857. Probably now the High Street there, as Marylebone and other lanes became the High Streets of the districts.

DENZHILL LANE, given by Harben, mentioned in L.C.C. deeds Harben Bequest 1700–1800 as being in the Parish of All Hallows-the-Less in the Ward of Dowgate in 1719.

Of Dirty Lanes, Dodsley gives ten—one in or near each of the following places: Blackman Street, Brewer's Street, High Holborn, Hoxton, Long Acre, Mint (Southwark), Shoreditch, Stoney Lane, Strand, and Old Palace Yard (Westminster).

I have failed to trace those in Shoreditch, Brewer Street and the Mint; but have accounted for seven.

The present Great Suffolk Street, Borough, is set down as Dirty Lane in a map of 1720, a continuation of Gravel Lane as it is now. For the original of the 'Moonrakers' sign of a public-house which has been here for nearly a century, Mr. Larwood suggests one of the tales of the Wise Men of Gotham. A party of them saw the reflection of the moon in the water, when out one night. After due deliberation they decided it was a green cheese and so raked for it.

The last of the Barber-surgeons lived in this street and died there about 1821. Mr. John Timbs said his name was Middlewich, and, 'renovare dolorem, had a vivid recollection of his dentistry!'

At the junction of this Dirty Lane with the old Southwark Bridge Road were Finch's Grotto Gardens, a famous Georgian resort, burned down in 1796. After the rebuilding a sculptured stone in the wall stated

> Here herbs did grow
> And flowers sweet,
> But now 'tis called
> Saint George's Street.

Another Dirty Lane in the Borough ran from Park Street to New Rents (now part of Catharine Street) across Stoney Street (or Lane, as it then was). The continuation of Dirty Lane was Foul Lane, to High Street, Borough, where it came out opposite St. Thomas Street. The lanes have been wiped out by the Borough Market. Counter Lane is now Counter Court. According to a book of hackney-coach fares, 1801, Dirty Lane, Hoxton Street, was between 'Land of Promise' and the 'King's Arms'.

Walcott's *Westminster* states that the previous thorough-fare formed under provisions of Act 23, George II, 1750, to Abingdon Street (which runs parallel to the Thames from Old Palace Yard to Millbank Street) was a 'narrow lane, pestered with coaches, narrow and inconvenient', and was aptly called Dirty Lane. The south gate of the Palace was in ST. MARGARET'S LANE. Dodsley gives a 'WHITE HART LANE, Broadway, Westminster'. I have not been able to trace it.

He gives also a WOOLSTAPLE LANE at New Palace Yard, where the Woolstaple was held.

A WOOL ACRE LANE is shown in Rocque's 1763 map as off Deptford Road, nearly opposite POT LANE.

Dirty Lane, Leicester Fields, was between Castle Street (demolished in the making of Charing Cross Road) and St. Martin's Lane by the Churchyard east; afterwards— in 1708—called Heming's Row.

The last house was pulled down in 1889. Until 1851, on an old wooden house at the west end of the Row, near the second-floor window, was to be seen the name of the street and the date 1680.

In John Overton's 1706 map the present Green Street is marked Dirty Lane.

In Strype's 1720 map the first turning on the right in Long Acre from Drury Lane is named Dirty Lane. It is called Charles Street in 1829 and 1840 maps. Arne Street now. In Butler's *Hudibras* we have

> He mounted Synod men, and rode 'em
> From Dirty Lane to Little Sodom.

Little Sodom was NEWTONER'S LANE (now Newton Street).

The list of hackney-coach fares for 1801 says that Dirty Lane, Kingsland Road, was 16 poles in length, and between the Workhouse and the Kingsland Turnpike, 4 furlongs 9 poles from Union Street.

Dirty Lane in the Strand has been previously written about.

DIGGS LANE is given in the Post Office *London Street Directory for* 1881 as being in Upper Richmond Road, Putney. Can find no trace of it, but in that road I find PUTNEY PARK, PRIORY, DYER'S and GIPSY LANES, no one of which is in the 1881 list.

There was another Gipsy Lane off WEST END LANE.

All that remains of the name of DISTAFF LANE is between 6 and 8 Cannon Street.

The old lane has been absorbed by that street, but a subsidiary street, previously known as LITTLE DISTAFF LANE, running into Knightrider Street, now preserves the old name.

In Hollars' engraving of 1666 Distaff Lane is called Maidenhead Lane.

Cordwainers' (Shoemakers') Hall, which was at one

time in Distaff Lane, remains, but is now numbered 7 Cannon Street on the north side.

By example of the King of Bohemia's daughter Anne, whom Richard II married, the English had used piked shoes, tied to their knees with silken hose, or silver or gilt chains. In Edward IV's reign it was enacted that beaks of shoone and boots should not pass the length of 2 inches, upon pain of cursing by the clergy, and by parliament to pay 20s. for every pair. And every cordwainer that shod any man or woman on the Sunday to pay 30s.

Stow says the lane was originally called DISTAR LANE. He mentions having read in a record dated 1436–7 of a brewery called the Lamb there. He remarks that 'on the south side of this Distar Lane, is also another lane called Distar Lane which runneth down to Knightrider Street, or Old Fish Street'.

In John Randulf's will, 1258, it is spelled DISTAVELANE. Walter de Nottingham, fishmonger, for 24 marks out of which his debts and legacies were to be paid, gives and assigns (in 1271) his house in DISTAFLANE to Margaret, his daughter.

A pound of cumin seed annual quit rent issuing from a tenement held by Nicholas Madefray in Distaflane was bequeathed to John Randolf de Ashlee by Wm. de Isyldon in 1349.

This lane had another name; for Stow says in describing the boundaries of Bread Street Ward . . . 'by the west end of Mayden Lane or Distar lane'. Again, 'On the west side of Friday Street is Mayden lane so named of such a sign, or Distaffe lane for Distar lane'.

DOLITTLE LANE, now called Knightrider Court, is just

a passage of some half-dozen houses between Knightrider Street and Carter Lane by No. 11, the back of Messrs. Cook Son & Co.'s back premises. In 1314 Walter de Hakeneye left to his son land in DOLYTELANE in the parish of St. Mary Magdalen.

Ben Jonson mentions this lane in his *Magnetick Lady*:

> I know the gentlewoman,
> Alderman Parrot's widow, a fine speaker,
> She dwelt in Dolittle Lane, a top o' the hill here.

In his *Masque of Christmas*:

> I had him by my first husband,
> He was a smith, forsooth, we dwelt in
> Dolittle Lane then.

Dolittle Rents are in Carter Lane.

From Knightrider Street to Thames Street ran PETER HILL LANE. PETRES LANE in 1375 and Peter's Hill now. The Abbot of St. Mary in York had a large, ancient house here on the east side.

ST. PETER'S LANE is mentioned in a will, 1349, of Wm. de Watford, fishmonger, who demised a house here to the Church of St. Peter-the-Less, for the maintenance of a chantrey, provided the parson of the said church, or the parishioners of same, pay to his executors the sum of twenty pounds. Stow said the only matter of note he could find in the lane were the almshouses on the west side founded by David Smith, embroiderer, for six poor widows, whereof each to have twenty shillings a year. The lane is named after the small parish church of St. Peter, called parva, or little.

OLD EXCHANGE LANE (now Old 'Change) is also out of

Knightrider Street and was so called because the King's
Exchange was there, for the receipt of bullion to be coined.

PETER'S LANE is a very short turning from St. John
Street, West Smithfield, to Cowcross Street. On the wall
of the Queen's Head Tavern which stood at the corner
of the lane and St. John Street was a stone tablet with the
inscription

opposite this Place Hicks Hall formerly stood, 1 mile 1
furlong from the Standard in Cornhill, 4 furlongs 205
yards from Holborn Barrs down Holborn, up Snow Hill,
Cow Lane and through Smithfield.

DOG KENNEL LANE is now Hill of the same name (a
continuation of GROVE LANE, Camberwell), in which is
the East Dulwich Sports Ground.

DOG LANE, old Fivefoot Lane, Southwark, is now
Tanner Street, and late Russell Street.

DISTILLERY LANE, the Hammersmith Distillery Co.,
runs from Fulham Palace Road to Elmdale Street,
Hammersmith.

DOLLIS HILL LANE is off the Edgware Road.

DOVE LANE is now Dove Court, between Old Jewry and
Grocers' Hall Court.

DUKE'S LANE is at 39 Church Street, Kensington.

CHAPTER X

Eaton Lane is at 21 Ebury Street, Pimlico, to Buckingham Palace Road, and like Eaton Square takes its name from Eaton Hall, Cheshire, the Duke of Westminster's seat. Large's *Way about London* gives Eaton Lane North and Eaton Lane South.

Eldea Lane was at Upper Millbank.

Electric Lane, from Coldharbour Lane to Atlantic Road, Brixton.

Engeron Lane is shown in Rocque's 1763 map as having been off Kingston Road (now Wandsworth Road). It seems to be identical with Thorne and Mawbey Streets, from Wandsworth Road to South Lambeth Road.

There were three Falcon Lanes: one at Falcon Stairs (Falcon Stairs were at Bankside); a second off Maiden Lane, Southwark, and another off High Street, Battersea.

Farm Lane is at Vanstone Place, Walham Green, not far from where on the south side of Fulham Road is now Waterford Road, once part of Sands-end-lane which is its continuation. This old lane was then the eastern boundary of Eel-Brook Common.

Felipeslane was an old spelling of Philip Lane. Peter de Frowick had shops in Fishmonger Lane in Henry VIII's time. Was that the present Fishmongers' Hall Street at 107 Upper Thames Street?

FIVE BELLS LANE is, in an 1881 *London Street Directory*, at Clifton Road, New Cross. The latter runs from Asylum Road to Pomeroy Street.

At No. 20 Buckingham Palace Road next to St. Philip's Church is FLASK LANE.

FLOWER LANE was at Mill Hill.

FYTRILANE is mentioned in the 1324 Will of John de Ludgarshale, who demised tenements in this lane 'and elsewhere in the parishes of St. Olave and St. Sepulchre'.

Is this identical with VITERILANE, supposed to be OLD LANE, mentioned in Thomas de Somersete's Will of 1294, in which he left to his daughter Katharine houses in the parish of St. Sepulchre without Newgate in Old Lane?

GARRATT LANE (connecting Wandsworth with Tooting) after the hamlet of that name which in Queen Elizabeth's time consisted of a single house called 'The Garrett' or, as Lyson says, 'The Garvet'. The mock elections for the 'borough of Garratt' were famous. Samuel Foote immortalized them, in 1761, in a farce—'The Mayor of Garratt'—which was put on the stage at the Haymarket Theatre.

The old GAYSPUR LANE is now Aldermanbury. St. Alphage Church, at the north-west corner, was rebuilt in 1777 on the site of a house of nuns, which, in 1329, being greatly decayed, William Elsing, mercer, began in place thereof the foundation for a hospital for one hundred blind men. This house was afterwards called a priory, or hospital, of St. Mary the Virgin, which, with the prior's and canon's house, with other lodgings, was subsequently made a dwelling-house. On the eve of Christmas, 1541, Sir John Williams, master of the King's jewels, was living here. At about 7 p.m. a great fire commenced in the gallery and the whole house was soon in flames, whereby many of the King's jewels were destroyed, and more (as was said) embezzled.

Stephen de Hale, felmongere, spells this lane GAYSPORE-LANE in his will, 1322, in which he left a tenement here to his wife Matilda for life.

Rents in GERMAYNESLANE and in Thames Street held by Arnold Tedmar were left in the will of Wm. de St. Alban, Rector of St. Mary de Kenardyntone (Kennington in Kent), in 1313, to be sold.

GIN LANE existed in Hogarth's imagination and was introduced by him in his well-known engraving as being in the parish of St. Giles-in-the-Fields. In the background he has drawn St. George's Church, Bloomsbury.

James de St. Edmund, in his will in 1313, mentions GOFAIRELANE in the parish of St. Swithens.

GOVAYRLANE is the spelling in the will, 1339, of John de Preston, corder, and GOVERESLANE in a draper's (Geoffrey le Botiller) will dated 8 December 1348.

GRANGE LANE, Bermondsey, would have been a lane leading to the old Abbey of the Cluniacs mentioned in Domesday, where it was stated that there was 'woodland' round about for the 'pannage' of a certain number of hogs; a 'new and fair church with twenty acres of meadow'.

GOODMAN'S LANE, now Yard, runs from the Tower end of the Minories to Mansell Street.

GOPHER LANE was on the east side of Bush Lane, Cannon Street.

GORDON HOUSE LANE (now Road) is off Highgate Road.

GREEN LANES, as now, is from Highbury New Park to

Newington Green. As of old in Rocque's 1763 map, Green Lanes included the present Mathias and Boleyn Roads, coming out at Kingsland Road below Castle Lane (now Crossways) already referred to.

Dodsley gives a Green Lane at Lambeth, and another at Tottenham Court Fields.

Albany Street, Regent's Park, was previously Green Lane.

GREEN'S LANE, Strand, was on the south-east side of and near Hungerford Market. The site is now covered by Charing Cross Railway Station. Sir Edmund Berry Godfrey was (according to the rate books of St. Martin's), a wood merchant in this lane. In Rocque's, 1763 map the Edgware Road end of Harrow Road north of Paddington Green is called Green Lane.

Large's *Way about London* mentions a GREEN COAT LANE as being the sixth on the right in Francis Street, Vauxhall Road. Probably the present Row of the same name is it.

GROVE LANE in Lambeth Marsh, east side of the Pear Tree public-house, mentioned in 1816 *Topography of London*, is now Cornwall Road. There is a Grove Lane at Stoke Newington.

GROVE STREET LANE in 1840 map is now Victoria Park Road on the west side leading to Hackney Wick.

GUN LANE (now Grenade Street), Three Colts' Lane (now Street), Limehouse, is now shortened. The eastern portion was demolished in making the West India Dock Road.

GUNMAKER'S LANE, Old Ford, E.3, is given in the *Names of Streets and Places in the London Postal Area for* 1920. I am not able to trace it.

In Isabella de Basinges' will of 1297 she bequeathed to her daughter houses in HADESTOKESLANE in the parish of St. Michael Queenhithe. In the earliest list of Aldermen for the City of London is the name of William de Hadestok as Alderman of the Tower Ward. The list is not dated, but there is good reason to conjecture it to have been about 1285–6, the fourteenth of Edward I. This may account for the name of the lane.

HAGBUSH LANE started in the ancient north road into Upper Holloway at the foot of Highgate Hill and went in that direction to Hornsey. From the mud cottage in it, it proceeded between Paradise House, the residence of Mr. Grieg, the engraver, and the Adam and Eve public-house, in the Holloway back road, and by circuitous windings approached London at the distance of a few feet on the eastern side of the City Arms public-house, in the City Road, and continued towards Old Street, St. Luke's. It did not communicate anywhere with the other long lane, leading from Battle-bridge to the top of Highgate Hill, called Maiden Lane.

Marked in an 1816 map, HIGLER'S LANE was a curly lane from the old St. George's Road (now Blackfriars Road) to the New Cut, coming out at the back of the Old Vic or the Victoria Hall as it first was. It is now Webber Street.

From Ball's Pond Turnpike to Highbury Grove was HOPPING LANE, so called from a few acres of land at the corner of Ball's Pond (afterwards Barr's Nursery, now St. Paul's Terrace) called The Hoppinge.

HORNEY LANE was from Neckinger to the Grange, which was between this lane and Spa Road.

HORN'S LANE was at Shoreditch.

In HARP LANE (previously 'Hart', says Stow)—from 18 Great Tower Street to 77 Lower Thames Street—an old house rich with wood carvings used to be shown as Whittington's, but he must have lived in his own parish of St. Michael Paternoster, most likely on the spot where was afterwards built his college, on the north side of the church. Baker's Hall is in this lane. This was the dwelling-house in which John Chicheley, Chamberlain of London (brother of Henry, Archbishop of Canterbury and founder of All Souls', Oxford), entertained Henry of Agincourt and his bride Katharine with such unusual magnificence that the King was astonished. When describing Cross Lane as running between Harp Lane and St. Dunstan's Hill, I omitted to mention that this hill was earlier known as a lane. In 1329 Lucy le Taverner left to Simon le Dallinge tenements in the parish of St. Dunstan towards the Tower in DUN-STONESLANE.

HART'S LANE, Bethnal Green Road, is now included in Barnet Grove. The latter at one time only extended from Columbia Street to Gossett Street.

At the junction of Love Lane, Bankside, and the present Sumner Street is still part of the old HOLLAND LANE (now Street), famous in the time of James I—the notorious 'stew' here being much frequented by his court, especially by George Villiers, the royal favourite, if we are to believe a tract entitled *Holland's Leaguer*. The peculiar inhabitants of this lane, Love Lane and Bankside were known as the 'Winchester Birds' from the propinquity of the palace of the Bishops of Winchester.

As far back as 1162 Parliamentary ordinances were issued for the governing of the Stew-holders in Southwark under the direction of the Lord Bishop of Winchester. No single woman was to be kept against her will, and all were to be 'voyded out of the lordship on Sundays and other holidays'. The number of stew-houses was, at that time, eighteen, reduced to twelve in the reign of Henry VII.

The poor women living in these houses, though licensed by the bishop, were not allowed Christian burial, but their dead bodies were cast into unconsecrated graves at a spot called the Crossbones in Redcross Street. Henry's son, when Richard I, issued a proclamation to his subjects enjoining them to avoid the Stews as being an abominable place.

Part of Holland Lane had previously been called the Green Walk.

There was a HOLLOWAY LANE in Whitechapel. It ran from Union Street, Whitechapel Road, to Greenfield Street, passing Plumtree Street on its left. Union Street has been renamed Adler Street. Holloway Lane has ascended to the dignity of Street, but has decreased in length; now extending only from Adler Street to Mulberry (late Plumtree) Street.

In 1351 one John le Chandeler of JUWERIELANE was executor to his kinsman Roger de Mymmes, chandeler. This was the present Old Jewry—OLD JURY LANE. POOR JURY LANE, so marked in Noorthouck's 1772 map, is the present Jewry Street, Aldgate High Street to Crutched Friars; where after their readmission to this country, subsequent to their banishment by Edward I, the Jews settled, having previously made Old Jewry their abode.

In 1760 an Act was passed to widen the passage of Poor Jury Lane to 35 feet by setting back part of those houses on the East side beginning with a house on the north side of 'The Horse and Trumpet', and extending southward to Gould, or Gold, Square (now America Square) so as to range in a line with that end of the lane next Aldgate. For some reason that was never done.

The old WOODROFF LANE from Crutched Friars to Tower Hill is now Cooper's Row. This is spelled WODEROVELANE in a will of Henry called le Botiner of the year 1283-4.

JUBILEE LANE was the lower end of the present Jubilee Street and ran between Clark Street and Commercial Road East at the Halfway House. Jubilee Street runs up to the Mile End Road and embraces this lane and Mutton Lane. which used to be the name of the lane from Redman's Road to Commercial Road East according to an 1840 map. In a map dated 1829 the middle of the now Jubilee Street is marked North Street. Allen, in 1828, refers to a curious old document dated 1718 in which is mentioned JOLLY LANE in Bishop's Liberty, Lambeth. I have not been able to discover its whereabouts.

There had been, near the spot known as Kennington Cross, a royal residence since the Saxon times. Edward the Black Prince was a frequent visitor. The road by which he travelled from the river to the Manor House is still called Prince's Road here, and the royal palace is commemorated by Royal Road, Mansion House Street, etc. From Newington Butts to Kennington Road runs LOWER KENNINGTON LANE, continued on the opposite side of the road as UPPER KENNINGTON LANE, as far as Vauxhall Bridge.

KING'S COLLEDGE LANE is given as being near Bristol Street, Puddle Docks. In Noorthouck's *Baynard's Castle Ward*, map of 1772, the named lane on the west of that

P

Dock is marked QUEEN's COLLEDGE LANE, Bristol Street being the next lane west of it. There is another narrow lane shown west of Bristol Street and one east of Queen's Colledge Lane, but they are not named

LAMBART HILL LANE (now Lambeth Hill), Upper Thames Street, to 95 Queen Victoria Street, so called from the owner thereof, says Stow.

On the west side was Blacksmiths' Hall.

Dodsley gives a LAND OF PROMISE LANE at Hoxton.

LARKHALL LANE is off Surrey Place, Wandsworth Road.

LANGLEY LANE is off South Lambeth Road, the next lane to which is Lawn Lane, next to Vauxhall Gardens before coming to Fentiman Road. Another lane near here was SPRING LANE, nearly opposite the house and museum of Charles I's gardener, the Tradescants, which together were called 'Tradescant' Ark'. The garden was famous and was in existence in 1749.

LAVENDER LANE runs from the road of that name to Battersea Rise.

Another with a similar name in Rotherhithe Street near the Horseferry. There is a Lavender Dock between Pageant Stairs and East Ferry Stairs.

LE LANE was the old name of Dudley Street, Broad Street, St. Giles, now demolished. Two estates—Newlands and Lelane—came into the hands of the brotherhood of St. Giles' as well as the spitalcroft (16 acres) lying on the north side of the highway opposite the great gates of the hospital. At the north end of LINDSAY LANE, upon the site of the Committee rooms of the House of Commons, was a tavern called 'Heaven'. Under the old Exchequer Chamber were two subterranean passages called 'Hell' and 'Purgatory'.

Butler, in *Hubidras*, mentions the first as False Heaven at the end of Hell. Old Fuller says he was informed that this 'Hell' was appointed a prison for the King's debtors, who never were freed thence until they had paid the uttermost farthing. The proverb is since applied to moneys paid into the Exchequer—irrecoverable, upon what pretence or plea whatever!

The present Abingdon Street, Old Palace Yard, was previously named Lindsay Lane; at the south-west end of which was Lindsay House, afterwards the residence of the Earl of Abingdon. Hence the change in the name.

Dodsley gives a LINTON LANE at Newington Butts. In an 1840 map it is marked Linton Street, now changed to Gurney Street.

LION-IN-THE-WOOD LANE or Paradise Road is mentioned in the *History of the Parish of Lambeth*, 1828. There is a Lion Street two turnings from Gurney Street in New Kent Road.

In Large's *Way About London*, OSBORNE'S LANE is described as being off New Kent Road down Rodney Place on the right, through Trafalgar Place, Salisbury Place to the first turning on the left past Cottage Row. Comparing maps, I find Rodney Place is now Road, which, wiping out Trafalgar Place and Hawksbury Place, continues past Flint Street to Elsted Street. This latter was Park Place, the next turning to Flint Street. No trace of Osborne's Lane or Cottage Row.

In a will of 1310 Alan de Horemede bequeaths to his daughter Felicia a tenement in Holebourne, and to his daughter Agnes three shops in LITTLE LANE (in venella parva). Can find no trace of this. It is mentioned in Nicholson's *New View*, etc.—1708.

LOMBARD LANE, Pleydell Court to Essex Street, Bouverie Street, according to the P.O. Directory—a very small, narrow turning.

LONGWICH LANE was on the east side of St. Pancras' Church. Norden, in the *Speculum Britannica*, says:

the old and auncient highwaye to High Bernet from Port Poole, now Gray's Inn, as also from Clerkenwell, was through a lane on the east side of Pancras Church, called Longwich Lane, and from thence leaving Highgate on the west of it past the Tallingdone Lane. .. . . This auncient waye was refused of wayfaring men and carriers by reason of the deepness and dirty passage in the winter season.

Camden, in his *Britannia*, says this road was open in 1300.

Dodsley mentions a LOWER TURNING LANE at Shadwell.

LOWHALL LANE is east of Leyton Marsh to Low Hall Farm.

LUMBY HOUSE LANE I cannot trace.

Lavender Lane, Lavender Hill, is mentioned, but the only lane off that Hill is WIX'S LANE at No. 15.

MARIGOLD LANE was at Upper Ground, Virginia Street, St. George Street, near London Docks.

MARSH GATE LANE and MARSH LANE are given as at Hackney Marsh. In the will, dated 1317, of Roysia de Coventre, 'MEDELANE in the parish of St. James de Garlekherthe' is mentioned.

The lane which now runs from 87 Fore Street to Chiswell Street is erected on the site of the Moorfields—the old Moor or Moor outside the walls—and is called MOOR LANE accordingly. In 1875–80 it only extended as far as Ropemaker Street, the city boundary. Then it took in its con-

tinuation Type Street, which is kept in memory by Type
Court. In 1331 it was called LE MORELANE. In 1332 it
changed its sex and is referred to as la morelane (with a
small 'm', too!).

The Fen or Moorfield was a waste and unprofitable
ground, a most noisome and offensive place burrowed and
crossed with deep stinking ditches and noisome common
sewers, and was held impossible to be reformed. It was let
for four marks in the reign of Edward II. But in Henry V's
time Thos. Falconer, the Mayor, caused the wall of the city
to be broken towards the moor, and built the postern called
Moorgate for the ease of the citizens to walk that way upon
causeways towards Iseldon and Hoxton. Moorfields were
first drained in 1527; laid out into walks in 1606 and first
built upon late in the reign of Charles II. Shakespeare in
Henry IV has the following dialogue:

FALSTAFF. 'Sblood, I am as melancholy as a gib-cat, or
a lugged bear.
PRINCE HENRY. Or an old lion; or a lover's lute.
FALSTAFF. Yea, or the drone of a Lincolnshire bagpipe.
PRINCE HENRY. What sayest thou to a hare, or the
melancholy of Moor ditch?

Between the Moor ditch on the south and the gardens of
Moorfield on the north almost to Moorgate was POSTERN
LANE, at the end of which lane was a potworker's house.
This lane was so named because there was a door at each
end of it to be shut at night. The Potteries were in Fore
Street. I have two small engravings showing Fore Street
then—two-storied cottages with lattice-windowed dormers
in the red-tiled roofs. The cottages seem to be whitewashed.

There is a POTTERY LANE at Notting Hill—the first

turning on the left in Portland Road, Holland Park Avenue.

NEATHOUSE LANE was off Ranelagh Road, Pimlico.

Oak Lane, Three Oak Lane, and Elms Lane have been mentioned. NINE ELMS LANE runs from Wandsworth Road to Battersea Park Road, a little way up which is STEWART'S LANE.

OLDFIELD LANE was the western end of the present Roman Road from Grove Road, Victoria Park.

OLD OAKE LANE is off Uxbridge Road.

NORTH END LANE (now Road) at the commencement of the last century was a country lane winding between market gardens. It deserves mention because of its many famous former residents. Foote, the dramatist and comedian, lived at the Hermitage—the site of which was afterwards occupied by Lovibond's Cannon Brewery at the corner of Lillie Road and the lane. At the opposite corner lived Bartolozzi, the artist, and father of Madame Vestris. Sir E. Lytton Bulwer was another resident. Cheeseman the engraver, Edmund Kean the actor, Copley and Cipriani the artists, all lived in this lane. Also Samuel Richardson, author of *Clarissa Harlowe*, etc. Here in his garden, in which were some fine cedars, he entertained many literary and other celebrities, including Dr. Johnson and Boswell.

From 180 North End Lane to Normand Lane was Star Lane (now Road). There were two more Star Lanes—off Barking Road and at Canning Town.

OLD MANOR LANE, Rotherhithe Old Road, was called WICK LANE in Bacon's map (no date, but before the Tower Bridge is shown). I here make a protest against the non-dating of atlases and maps.

In an old directory for London OLIPHANT'S LANE, Rotherhithe, and OLIVER'S LANE, Shoreditch, are mentioned. I cannot trace them.

At St. Peter's Road to Upper Mall, Hammersmith, is an OIL MILL LANE.

PARK LANE, Piccadilly—once the longest lane in London, now beaten by Brick Lane, as previously mentioned—was formerly called TYBURN LANE because it led to Tyburn. The name was introduced in the rate-books of St. Martin's-in-the-Fields for the first time in 1679. It was then called Tyburn Road. In 1686 it was called Tyburn Lane. In Queen Anne's time it was but a desolate lane. As late as 1722 there were only a few buildings—Mayfair Row and Hay Hill Row—from the lane to the south wall of Lord Chesterfield's garden in Curzon Street; the rest was all open spaces and fields, and the lane was just a country lane, shaded by trees, winding its quiet way along by the palings of the park which belonged to the monastery of St. Peter, Westminster—being the site of the ancient manor of Hyde —until it was conveyed in 1536 to Henry VIII. In 1550 the French Ambassador hunted there and in 1578 the Duke Casimir shot a doe from amongst 300 other deer in the Park. The latter was sold, by order of Parliament, in 1652 for £17,000, the deer extra.

Evelyn in the following year writes:

I went to take the aire in Hide Park, when every coach was made to pay a shilling and every horse sixpence by the sordid fellow (Anthony Dene), of St. Martins-in-the-Fields), who had purchased it of the State, as they were called.

At the beginning of the eighteenth century hardly a house

was built in the lane, but the sons of George Bushwell, the sculptor who adorned the old Temple Bar, lived there in an unfinished house with neither staircase nor doors, but choked up with unfinished statues and pictures. The Elgin Marbles were first exhibited in this country at Lord Elgin's house—the large one at the south-west corner afterwards inhabited by H.R.H. the Duchess of Gloucester. This was the house Byron called 'a stone shop' and 'general mart for all the mutilated blocks of art'. But the British Museum bought them for £35,000.

Park Lane was the most fashionable thoroughfare in London and some of the most noble mansions were built there. Now—well, I expect there will be a row of shops there soon. There is a Park Lane, or what remains of one, at 31 New Street, Marylebone, and another at 35 Albion Road, Stoke Newington. There was a Park Lane running west out of Church Street, Chelsea, leading into old Chelsea Park. It now appears to form part of Elm Park Road.

Rocque's 1747 map shows a PAUL's CHAIN LANE at St. Paul's Churchyard on the south side. Dodsley mentions it.

ST. PAUL'S LANE runs south out of Rotherhithe Street by the girls' school.

Schoolhouse Lane is at 36A, Brook Street, St. George Street, to Broad Street.

The Schoolhouse Lane mentioned by Dodsley as off Ailesbury Street was where the Parish Schools founded in 1700 stood before they removed to Amwell Street. Schoolhouse Yard still remains.

SCHOOL LANE at Jamaica Road, Rotherhithe, I have not traced. Dodsley gives it.

A PAWNBROKER'S LANE is mentioned in Large's *Way*

About London as being on the left of High Street, Stoke Newington.

The original name of Bath Street, St. Luke's, Old Street leading to Perilous Pond, was PEST-HOUSE LANE. The Pond was a spring which overflowing its banks, caused a dangerous pool in which many persons were drowned. It was afterwards named Peerless Pool by its temporary proprietor, in 1743, who had it properly filled in and enclosed.

Ben Jonson in *Christmas his Masque* has:

> This carol plays, and has been in his days
> A chirping boy and a kill-pot.
> Kit cobbler it is, I'm a father of his,
> And he dwells in the lane called Fill-pot.

Such is his spelling of the lane in Fenchurch Street named after the Mayor of London in 1378—Sir John Philpot, who lived in it and was the owner thereof. In 1623, when the Fleet was fitting out to bring Prince Charles and the Infanta from Spain, the Commodores of the Navy dated their letters from PHILPOT LANE.

PILGRIM LANE was probably the present street of that name and had some connection with the neighbouring Friary of the Dominicans.

A Pilgrim's Lane is off Rosslyn Hill, Hampstead.

In an old directory for London PIE CORNER LANE is mentioned as being at West Smithfield.

In Large's *Way About London*, PLOUGH LANE is given as being the third on the left past Notting Hill Gate. That would be the present Johnson Street, or, not counting the passage, Campden Hill Road. The 'Plough' is on the opposite side of the main road.

Another Plough Lane is given at Limehouse, and yet another at Homerton, neither of which can I trace.

In Rocque's 1763 map is PODDER'S LANE, Lambeth, off Kingston (now Wandsworth) Road. Next east is ENGERON LANE. These are now Priory and Lansdowne Roads leading to South Lambeth Road.

Puerto Bello and its harbour in the Gulf of Mexico was taken from the Spaniards in 1739, by Admiral Vernon. To commemorate his victory a Mr. A. Adams, who owned a farm in the neighbourhood of Notting Hill, called it Porto Bello Farm, and to the lane leading east (which had previously been known as Green Lane) he gave the name PORTO BELLO LANE. It is now Porto Bello Road. SCRUBBS LANE, from Harrow Road to Shepherd's Bush, is not very far from here.

At the end of the eighteenth century, Mrs. Cornelys, of Soho Square fame, took an old mansion—Knightsbridge Grove—under the assumed name of Mrs. Smith, for society to drink new asses' milk. The approach to this, a little west of Wilton Place, was PORTER'S LANE. It is now William Street.

In the will of Simon de Parys, mercer, dated 1324, he left shops, etc., in PUPPEKIRTELESLANE in the parish of St. Pancras. POPCURTLESLANE and PUPEKIRTILLANE are mentioned in a thirteenth-century will of Thomas de Basinge.

Large gives a PACK HORSE LANE, Caledonian Road, Lower Holloway, as being off Upper George's Place, and the first turning on the right past Grove Street.

From Cardinal Place to Charlwood Road, Putney, is QUILL LANE.

RATONE LANE is mentioned in a manuscript of the year 1327. In a view taken of the precincts of the Thames in 1344 the lane called RATONES LANE is described, in the parish of St. Michael's, Queenhithe, as a common lane on which a trespass had been committed by the Abbot of Lesnes contrary to custom of the city, and it was said further that a course of water which ought to run through the lane had been impeded by the predecessors of Thomas de Stemforde to the public hurt. His name seems rather apposite.

REDFIELD LANE is at 111 Earl's Court Road.

EARL'S COURT LANE is given by Large as being the first turning on the right in Richmond Road.

RIDING HOUSE LANE (now Street) is off Great Portland Street.

REGENT'S LANE at Preston's Road, Poplar.

ROOMLAND LANE is mentioned by Dodsley as being in Thames Street. Off the wharves in Upper and Lower Thames Street lay ships of all nations. This was evidently one of the lanes leading to the stairs between the quays, in which lived the seafaring folk and those who worked for them and for the merchants. These quays, landing-places, and land adjoining went, in olden times, by the picturesque name of Roomland—that is to say, round Queenhithe, Dowgate, Billingsgate, etc., whereon goods might be discharged.

Mention is made of houses built upon la Romeland by St. Michael, Queenhithe, in 1311.

Ralph de Beri, cordwainer, left property in ROPERES-LANE in 1313. It was usually called the Ropery, situate in the parish of All Hallows the Great, thence known as

All Hallows in the Ropery, or All Hallows at the Hay, from its proximity to a hay wharf.

Dodsley gives a ROPER LANE as being off Crucifix Lane, Barnaby Street, Southwark; Barnaby Street being now Bermondsey Street.

In an old directory for London is given SIX BELLS LANE, Bucklersbury.

John le Wilde, mason, in 1316 bequeathed 2s. annual rent issuing from a tenement in a LANE called LE SPITEL-DICHE towards the maintenance of the fabric of S. Sepulchre's church.

'SOUTHAMLANE, in Temestreete', is mentioned in a 1383 letter book in connection with a felony. This would be SPITTLE LANE at the Priory and Hospital of St. Mary Spittle, founded by Walter Brune and Rosia his wife, for canons regular. The first stone was laid in 1197. It was built on Spittlefields, of old time called Lolesworth field. In Nicholson's *New View of London*, 1708, a LOLESWORTH'S LANE is mentioned. It was broken up in about 1576 for clay to make brick; when many earthen pots, called urnæ, were found full of ashes and burned human bones. In every pot was also one piece of copper money with the inscription of the Emperor then reigning: some of Claudius, of Nero, of Antoninus Pius, Trajanus, and others. Phials, glasses, crystals, dishes and cups of a fine red-coloured earth, with Roman letters printed on the bottoms, and some images; stone coffins containing bones, and a curious pot of white earth, small, in the shape of a hare squatting; between the ears was the mouth of the pot.

In addition to the Ship Lane which was the next west

St. Martins Lane

lane to Shire Lane by the new Law Courts, there is a Ship Lane at Warple Road, Wandsworth; another off Kennington Road and a third in Queen Street, Hammersmith.

Rocque gives a ST. JOHN'S WOOD LANE. In his 1763 map Lising Green is shown, and a road, which evidently is now Lisson Grove, continued to the Hill House. At Punker's Barn starts St. John's Wood Lane, which turns round to the right, probably the top of the present St. John's Wood Road.

ST. MARTIN'S LANE, Westminster, shares with Aldersgate Street, Great Queen Street, Lincoln's Inn Fields and Covent Garden the distinction of having had built in it some of the first brick houses erected in London. These were built from 1618 to 1636. In about the year 1600 houses were being built upon the ground abutting the lane, for letters patent of Charles I gave to St. Martin's parish one acre of land on the west side of St. Martin's Lane nearly opposite the church for a burial-ground 'with the rents of the houses standing thereon'. But there is a Proclamation of Henry VIII's in the library of the Society of Antiquaries, dated 1546, to the effect that the 'Games of Hare, Partridge, Pheasant and Heron' were to be 'preserved from Westminster Palace to St. Giles's-in-the-Fields, etc.'. The old church of St. Martin's-in-the-Fields was in a state of ruin in Henry VIII's time and was not rebuilt until James I took it in hand. Then this lane was called WEST CHURCH LANE. The upper part of the lane was originally called the 'Terrace'. The whole of the lower part was demolished for widening the Strand and the Charing Cross Act received Royal Assent on 31 May 1826. For effecting the principal improvements 515 houses and buildings in and near Charing Cross, St. Martin's Lane and the Strand were required, of an estimated value of £748,792 12s. 10d.—found to be really £843,950 4s. 9d. The purchase of the old Golden Cross Hotel was the heaviest item, concluded in December 1827, when these premises, three houses in St. Martin's Lane and two houses and workshops in Frontier Court, were bought from George Howard and others for £30,000.

The lane has had many notable residents. Sir Theodore Mayerne, physician to James I, lived on the west side in 1613: Daniel Mytens, the painter, resided here from 1622–34: Prince Charles gave him his home for twelve years at a peppercorn rent of sixpence a year.

Earl of Stirling, 1631–2; Sir Walter Raleigh's son, 1636–8 and 1664; Sir John Suckling; the Earl of Shaftesbury; Dr. Thomas Tenison, Vicar of St. Martin's, afterwards Archbishop of Canterbury; Sir James Thornhill; Sir Joshua Reynolds; Fuseli, were all inhabitants.

Coutts' Banking House was established here in the reign of Queen Anne by Middleton, a goldsmith. Slaughter's Coffee House was a favourite resort here.

The office of the *London Gazette* was at No. 45. The *Gazette* was first published at Oxford when the Court was there during the Great Plague in London, and was called the *Oxford Gazette* until the return to town, when No. 24 became the *London Gazette*.

Just over a century has elapsed since the last disturbing and rearranging of the Charing Cross area. In another five years the completion of the London County Council's fourteen and a half millions traffic plan and the new bridge to replace Hungerford and the existing eyesore of the

railway bridge will again improve the amenities of the
neighbourhood; though I fancy we shall all miss the old
station and the replica of the cross erected to the memory
of Edward I's dear Queen—the 'chère reine' which some
people like to think is the derivation of 'Charing' Cross.

APPENDIX

Present Names.	*Old Names.*
Abbeyfield Road, Bermondsey .	Manor Lane
Abingdon Street, Westminster .	Lindsay Lane, Dirty Lane
Addle Street, City.	Addelane, Athelane
Albany Street, Regent's Park .	Green Lane
Aldermanbury	Gayspur Lane
All Hallows Lane, Upper Thames Street	Church Lane
Anchor Alley, Upper Thames Street	Anchor Lane, Palmer's Lane
Artillery Lane, Bishopsgate . .	Berewardes Lane, Hog Lane
Ashburn Place, South Kensington	Atwood Lane
Assembly Passage, Mile End Road	Mutton Lane
Avenue Road, Camberwell . .	Windmill Lane
Avery Row, Brook Street . .	South Molton Lane
Barnet Grove, Bethnal Green .	Hart's Lane
Barnsbury Road with Albany Street	Barnsbury Lane
Bath Street, St. Luke's . . .	Pest-house Lane
Battle Bridge Lane	Mill Lane
Bell-Wharf Lane	Herbers Lane, Brikell's Lane, Emperor's Head Lane, Simpson's Lane
Ben Jonson Street, Mile End Road	Cow Lane, Beast Lane, Bull Lane
Billiter Street, City	Billiter Lane, Bell-zetar's Lane, Belhetereslane
Bingle's Road, Victoria Docks .	Bingle's Lane
Bishop's Road, Fulham . . .	Bishop's Lane
Botolph Lane	Bottle Lane

Present Names.	*Old Names.*
Boundary Street, Shoreditch .	Cock Lane, New Cock Lane
Bow Lane, Cheapside . . .	Hosier Lane, Cordwainer Street
Brecknock Road, Camden Town	Maiden Lane, Longwich Lane, Long-Hedge Lane
Brewers Lane, Upper Thames Street	Tennis-Court Lane
Brick Street, Piccadilly . . .	Brick Lane
Brompton Road	Brompton Lane
Bucknall Street, St. Giles's . .	Church Lane
Bull's Wharf Lane, Upper Thames Street	Pump Lane
Bush Lane, City	Carter's Lane, Chequer's Lane
Cable Street, Stepney . . .	Back Lane, Rosemary Lane
Carey Lane, City	Kery Lane
Carlisle Street, Lambeth . . .	Carlisle Lane
Carting Lane	Dirty Lane?
Castle Lane, Westminster . .	Cabbage Lane
Catherine Street, Borough . .	Dirty Lane
Central Street, St. Luke's . .	Brick Lane
Chancery Lane	Chancellor's Lane, Converts' Lane
Charing Cross Road	Hog Lane
Charles Street, Drury Lane . .	Lewknor's Lane
Charterhouse Street	Charterhouse Lane
Church Passage Old Jewry . .	Bordhawe Lane, Burdellane, Bordhangly Lane
Clapton Square	Bob's Hall Lane
Clarence Road, Clapton . . .	Back Lane
Cleveland Street, Mile End Road	Red Cow Lane
Cloak Lane, City	Horsebridge Lane
Coborn Road, Old Ford . .	Bearbinder Lane
College Street, City	College Lane, Elbow Lane
Commercial Road	Whitehorse Lane
Commercial Street	Rose Lane
Cornwall Road, Lambeth Marsh	Grove Lane
Corporation Row, Clerkenwell .	Corporation Lane
Craven Terrace, Paddington. .	Elms Lane
Creed Lane	Spurrier Row, Sporenereslane
Creek Street, Deptford . . .	Slaughter House Lane
Cressyngham Lane	Spittle Lane
Crisp Street	Poplar Lane

Present Names.	*Old Names.*
Cromwell Road, Kensington. .	Cromwell Lane
Cross Lane, St. Mary-at-Hill. .	Fowle Lane
Crossway, Stoke Newington . .	Cock and Castle Lane, Cork Lane
Czar Street, Deptford. . . .	Back Lane, Butt Lane
Dawes Road, Fulham. . . .	Dawes Lane
Devon's Road, Bow	Devon's Lane
Distaff Lane, City	Distar, Distavelane, Distaflane
Dove Court, Old Jewry . . .	Dove Lane
Duck's Foot Lane	Duke's foot-lane
Duckett Road, Stepney . . .	Duckett's Lane
Dudley Street, St. Giles's. . . (now demolished)	Le Lane
Earl's Court Road	Earl's Court Lane
East Street, Walworth . . .	East Lane
Edward Street, Deptford . . .	Loving Edward Lane
England's Lane, Hampstead . .	Ingram's Lane
Fetter Lane	Faitour Lane, Faytour Lane, Faitereslane
Field Lane, Clerkenwell . . .	Goldelane, Goldeslane, Gold Lane
Fleet Lane	St. Georges Lane, Little Old Bailey Lane
Flockton Street, Bermondsey. .	Salisbury Lane
Flood Street, Chelsea	Robinson's Lane
Foster Lane, City	Seint Uastes lane, St. Vedast's Lane
Frederick's Place	Gropecountelane
Friars Alley, Upper Thames Street	Fryer's Lane, Greenwich Lane
Frog Lane, Islington	Brick Lane
Fulborne Street, Whitechapel .	Greyhound Lane
Golden Lane, Barbican . . .	Golding Lane, Goldyng Lane
Grace Street, Poplar	Starch Lane
Great Hermitage Street, Wapping	Great Hermitage Lane
Great Suffolk Street, South-wark	Dirty Lane
Green Street, Leicester Square .	Dirty Lane
Grenade Street, Limehouse . .	Gun Lane
Gresham Street	Maiden Lane, Lad Lane, St Ann's Lane

Present Names.	*Old Names.*
Grocers' Hall Court, Poultry . .	Coneyhope Lane, Conynghop-lane
Grove Street, Deptford . . .	Grove Lane
Gurney Street, Newington Butts	Linton Lane
Gutter Lane, City	Godronelane, Guthron's Lane, Goderoneslane, Godereslane, Godronelane, Gother Lane, Goster Lane, Gudrunlane
Haggerston Road	Stonebridge Lane, Haggerston Lane
Hanbury Street, Spitalfields . .	Brown's Lane
Harp Lane, Thames Street . .	Hart Lane
Harrow Alley, Houndsditch . .	Harrow Lane
Hartwells Road, Dalston . . .	Hartwell's Lane
Heneage Lane	Innage Lane, Image Lane, Lousie or Lousy Lane, Louse Lane
High Timber Street	Dunghill Lane
Holland Street, Bankside . . .	Gravel Lane, Green Lane
Holloway Street, Whitechapel .	Holloway Lane
Hornsey Road	Du Val's Lane, Devil's Lane, Tallingdone Lane
Huggin Lane, Upper Thames Street	Hoggenlane, Hoggenelane, Spooner's Lane, Spuren Lane
Ironmonger Lane	Isemongerelane, Ysmongerelane
Ivy Lane	Ivilane, Yvieslane, Alsieslane, Fukemar Lane, Folkmares Lane, Folkmere Lane
Jubilee Street, Stepney . . .	Jubilee Lane, Mutton Lane
Kensington Place, Campden Hill	Brookfield Lane
King Edward Street, City . .	Stinkendelane, Stinking Lane, Chick Lane, Chickine Lane, Fowle Lane,
King Street, West Smithfield . .	Cow Lane
Knightrider Court	Dolittle Lane
Lambeth Hill, City	Lambert Hill Lane
Laurence Pountney Hill . . .	Duck's Foot Lane, Duke's foot-lane, Burford Lane, Green Lettuce Lane, Green Lattice Lane
Laurence Pountney Lane . . .	Lawrence Poulteney Lane
Lawrence Street, High Street, St. Giles's	Lawrence Lane

Present Names.	*Old Names.*
Lea Bridge Road	Pond Lane
Leinster Terrace, Paddington .	Craven Lane
Little Britain	Duck Lane
Little Paris Street, Lambeth . .	Love Lane
Love Lane, Shadwell	Cutthroat Lane
Love Lane, Monument Street .	Lucas Lane, Roape Lane, Roppe-lane
Lupus Street, Pimlico . . .	Cross Lane
Mack's Road	Mark's Lane
Magdalen Street, Bermondsey .	Maudlin Lane
Maguire Street, Horselydown .	New Gravel Lane, New Lane
Maiden Lane, King's Cross . .	Midden Lane, Dunghill Lane
Mantell Street, Islington . . .	Sermon Lane
Mark Lane	Mart Lane, Blanch Apleton
Martin's Lane, City	Lane of St. Martin Orgar, St. Martin's Lane
Middlesex Street	Petticoat Lane, Rosemary Lane, Hog Lane
Middleton Road, Kingsland Road	Fox Lane
Miles Lane, City	Lane of St. Michael de Candal-eviestrate, Seint Michleslane, Lane of St. Michael de Crooked Lane, St. Mighell's Lane
Mill Street, St. Saviour's Dock .	Mill Lane
Mincing Lane	Menionelane, Mangonelane, Mani-manelane, Monecheni-lane, My-niounlane
Morgan's Lane, Tooley Street .	Old Horselydown Lane
Morning Lane, Hackney . . .	Mourning Lane, Money Lane
New Kent Road	Corbett's Lane
New Park Street, Southwark . .	Maid Lane
Newton Street, High Holborn .	Newtoner's Lane, Little Sodom
Normand Road, North End Row	Normand Lane
Northumberland Avenue . .	Hartshorn Lane
Oat Lane	Oate Lane
Oldfield Road, Stoke Newington	Cutthroat Lane
Old Ford Road	Old Ford Lane, Coat's Lane
Old Jewry	Juwerislane, Colechirchelane
Old Manor Lane	Wick Lane
Outward Street	Ducking Pond Lane

Present Names.	*Old Names.*
Pakenham Street, Gray's Inn Road	Fifteenfeet Lane
Pancras Lane	Needler's Lane
Paris Street, Lambeth . . .	Love Lane
Park Lane	Tyburn Lane
Park Street, Canonbury . . .	Kettle Lane
Paternoster Row	Paternoster Lane
Penrose Street, Walworth. . .	West Lane
Peter's Hill	Peter Hill Lane, Petreslane
Plough Road, Deptford . . .	Plough Lane
Popham Road, Islington . . .	Frog Lane
Portobello Road, Notting Hill .	Portobello Lane, Green Lane
Prebend Street, Islington . .	Frog Lane
Princes Road, Vauxhall . . .	Workhouse Lane
Pudding Lane, City	Rother Lane, Red Rose Lane, Fynkeslane, Podyng Lane, Rederisgate Lane, Retheresgate Lane, Rotheresgates Lane, Redereslane, Redderisgate Lane
Queen Street, Cheapside . . .	Church Lane, Vanner's Lane, Broad Lane, Sopar Lane, Sopereslane, Soper's Lane
Queen's Head Street, Islington .	Queen's Head Lane, Almshouse Lane, Boon's Lane
Queen Victoria Street . . .	Distaff Lane, Maidenhead Lane, St. Thomas Lane, Pissing Lane, Turnbas Lane, Turnbase Lane
Raymond Street, Wapping . .	Meeting House Lane
Rectory Road, Stoke Newington	Shacklewell Lane
Red Mead Lane, Wapping . .	Red Maid Lane
Reverdy Street, Southwark Park Road	Tenter Ground Lane
Rheidol Terrace, Islington . .	Frog Lane
Rhodeswell Road	Rhodeswell Lane, Sermons Lane, Rogue's Lane
Rolt Street, Deptford	Coney Hall Lane
Rood Lane, City	Patten's Lane, St. Margaret Patten's Lane
Royal Mint Street.	Rosemary Lane
Seething Lane	Syvidlane

Present Names.	Old Names.
Selwood Terrace, Kensington .	Sallad Lane
Sermon's Lane, City	Sheremoniers Lane, Sermouneres Lane
Seymour Place, Marylebone . .	Stingo Lane, Bowling Green Lane
Sherborne Lane, City . . .	Share-borne Lane, Southborne Lane, Scire-burn Lane, Shitteborwelane, Shiteburnelane, Shiteburlane, ShitebourneLane
Shoe Lane, Fleet Street . . .	Sholane, Showell Lane, Scolane
Sise Lane	St. Sith's Lane, St. Osyth's Lane
St. Dunstan's Hill	Dunstoneslane
St. Martin's Lane, Westminster .	West Church Lane
St. Peter Street, Islington . .	River Lane
Stew Lane, Upper Thames Street	Hamond's Lane, Parkeris Lane
Sumner Street, Southwark . .	Maid Lane
Sutherland Street, Pimlico . .	Baker's Lane
Swan Lane	Ebgate Lane
Tanner Street, Bermondsey . .	Dog Lane, Fivefoot Lane
Three Cranes Lane, City . .	Painted Tavern Lane
Three Colt Street, Bethnal Green	Three Colt Lane
Tredegar Road, Old Ford . .	Bearbinder Lane
Trinity Church Passage, Fetter Lane	Feather-bed Lane
Umberstone Road, Commercial Road	Umberstone Lane
Union Road, Newington Causeway	Horsemonger Lane
Uverdale Road, Fulham . . .	Poole's Lane
Victoria Park Road, Hackney Wick	Grove Street Lane
Vine Street, Clerkenwell . . .	Mutton Lane
Water Lane, Great Tower Street	Sporiar Lane
Webber Street, New Cut . . .	Higler's Lane
West Street, St. Martin's Lane, Westminster	West Lane
Whitcomb Street, Pall Mall East	Hedge Lane
Whitefriars Street, Fleet Street .	Water Lane
William Street, Knightsbridge .	Porter's Lane
Woodpecker Road, Deptford. .	Trundley's Lane
Worship Street, Shoreditch . .	Hog Lane

Wyndham Road, Camberwell .	Bowyer Lane
York Road, King's Cross . .	Maiden Lane, Midden Lane, Longwich or Longhedge Lane
York Street, Westminster . .	Cabbage Lane

INDEX

R*

London Fields, 88
London Gazette, 222
London Lane, 84, 177, 192
London General Omnibus Company, 112
London Road Car Company, 112
London Stone, 33
London Street, 110
Long Acre, 30, 75, 78, 198
Long Lane, Borough, 19, 80
— — Smithfield, 22, 23
Long Street, Shoreditch, 19
Longhedge Lane, 54
Longwich Lane, 54, 212
Lothbury, 45, 46
Louerone Lane, 124
Louse Lane, 178
Lousie Lane, 178
Lousy Lane, 178
Love Lane, Aldermanbury, 17, 151
— — Bankside, 207
— — Brook Street, 17
— — Eastcheap, 15, 16, 31
— — Lambeth, 18
— — Marylebone, 18
— — Rotherhithe, 17
— — Southwark, 17, 101
— — Westminster, 17
Lovelace, Richard, 143
Lovell, Sir Thomas, 128
Love, Reynold, 16
Loving Edward Lane, 18
Lovken, John, 17
Lower Kennington Lane, 209
Lower Queen Street, 30
Lower Road, Islington, 109
Lower Thames Street, 12, 16, 207
Lower Turning Lane, 212
Lowhill Lane, 212
Lucas Lane, 16
Ludgate, 148, 149
Ludgate Circus, 61
Ludgate Hill, 50, 61
Lumby House Lane, 212
Lupus Street, 30
Lymbarnereslane, 59
Lymbrennereslane, 59
Lyneroune-lane, 124
Lyon's Wharf, 4
Lytton, Sir E. Bulwer, 214

Macaulay, Zachary, 43
Machyn, Henry, 8
Macklin Street, 30
Mack's Road, Bermondsey, 161
Madrigal Society, The, 148
Magdalen Street, 118
Magpye Lane, 77

Maguire Street, 99
Maid Lane, Borough, 56, 57, 101
— — Lambeth, 57
Maiden Lane, Garlick Hill, 54
— — Gresham Street, 45, 46, 47
— — Half Moon Street, 54
— — Holloway, 54
— — King's Cross, 4
— — Strand, 54, 55, 56
Maidenhead Lane, Bloomsbury, 57
— — E.C., 57, 198
Mail-coaches, annual procession, 112
Maize Row, 164
Mangonelane, 170
Manimanelane, 170
Manor Lane, 18
Manor of the Maze, 118
Manor of the Rose, The, 26, 27
Mansion House, 61
Mansion House Street, 209
Mantell Street, 90
Mare Street, 84, 87, 88, 109, 110
Marigold Lane, 212
Marigold Street, 31
Marine Coffee House, 43
Mark House Lane, 161
Mark Lane, 160, 181
Market Lane, Kennington, 161
— — St. James, 161
— — Shadwell, 161
Market Street, 111
— — St. James, 161
Marks Lane, 161
Marshalsea, The, 22
Marsh Gate Lane, 212
Marsh Lane, 212
Mart Lane, 160
Martin's Lane, 35
Marvell, Andrew, 55
Marylebone Gardens, 96
Marylebone, High Street, 91
Marylebone Lane, 18, 91, 92, 93, 94, 96
Marylebone Park, 94
Marylebone Street, 95
Mary, Queen of Scots, 161
Massingham, John, 49
Maudlin Lane, 118
Mawbey Street, 202
Mayerne, Sir Theodore, 222
Mayfield Road, 87
Mayfair Row, 215
Mayhew, Henry, 135
Maypole Alley, 77
Maypole Lane, 77
May's Lane, 119
Maze Lane, 119
Maze Pond, 119
Meadow Road, 86

BY THE SAME AUTHOR

HOW WE LIVED THEN

1914–1918 : A SKETCH OF SOCIAL AND DOMESTIC LIFE IN ENGLAND DURING THE WAR

By Mrs. C. S. PEEL

Fully illustrated from contemporary photographs.

Demy 8vo.   15s. net.

" Mrs. Peel has written a lively narrative, full of pleasant personal touches and authentic quotations from private letters, that has an immediate appeal and will doubtless become a useful footnote to the history of these times. The notes and illustrations dealing with women's fashions in dress are somehow very surprising and amusing. Mrs. Peel has put us into her debt once more by producing this timely and entertaining record."—*Times Literary Supplement.*

" On every page some vital fact is vivaciously recalled, and Mrs. Peel is to be congratulated on a book which is a vivid and faithful picture of a nation at war under modern conditions."—*Morning Post.*

" A sympathetic, balanced and well-illustrated chronicle of ' How We Lived Then, 1914–18,' has a twofold value. It fills up the gaps which render the nightmare as a whole extremely difficult to reconstruct and it provides for posterity an eloquent record of what actually happens to the social life of a modern state brought into comparatively mild relations with modern warfare."—*Punch.*

" Mrs. Peel's account, with its numerous comic or pathetic photographs, is well done and was well worth doing, for it records the extraordinary shifts of the civil population in time of war."—*Sphere.*

JOHN LANE THE BODLEY HEAD LTD., VIGO STREET, W.1

BIOGRAPHY AND MEMOIRS

PERSONALITIES AND POWERS

By KNUT HAGBERG, author of "Kings, Churchills, and Statesmen." Translated from the Swedish by ELIZABETH SPRIGG and CLAUD NAPIER.

Demy 8vo. 12s. 6d. net.

The Swedish writer, Dr. Knut Hagberg, won instant recognition from the British press and public with his volume of biographical studies "Kings, Churchills and Statesmen," and his book was everywhere praised as an extraordinarily penetrating and trenchant estimate of some of our leading public figures from a foreigner's point of view. His new volume of studies provides even more varied fare. Among English politicians he presents Melbourne, Disraeli, Gladstone, Parnell, Sir William Harcourt, Lord Balfour, and Lord Grey; and besides these, other essays deal with Lord Kitchener, Cecil Rhodes, Paul Deschanel, Ernest Renan, John Stuart Mill, Samuel Pickwick and Isabella d'Este.

THE DIARIES OF COLONEL THE HONOURABLE ROBERT FULKE GREVILLE, relating to the intimate and private life of George III

Edited by F. McKNO. BLADON.

Illustrated. Demy 8vo. 25s. net.

Robert Greville, brother of Charles Greville, and Equerry and Groom of the Bedchamber to King George III for 38 years, has left behind him an exceedingly interesting series of diaries, recording much which has not hitherto come to light of the intimate and personal daily life of his King at St. James's, Windsor, Kew and Weymouth. The author accompanied George III to Naval and Military Reviews, to meets of the Royal Stag Hounds and Lord Poulett's Harriers, and on informal visits to many private houses; he was in constant attendance upon him during his illness and insanity of 1788, and during his subsequent visits to Weymouth. All this he has recorded in interesting detail, together with incidents dealing with many other celebrities of the time.

ON THE TRAIL: Being My Reminiscences as a Cowboy.

By FRANK HARRIS, author of "The Man Shakespeare," "Montes The Matador," etc.

Crown 8vo. 7s. 6d. net.

To the generation of 1930 Frank Harris is already a legend. At 75 he sits on his balcony by the Mediterranean and remembers his youth. In the legend known to most of us he figures as the man of letters, the friend and companion of Whistler, Wilde and his great contemporaries, and as the author of some of the finest short stories in the English language. But before he was these things he was a cowboy on the western plains of America, whither he emigrated from Ireland, where he was born. And in this book he tells the story of his youthful experiences with the simplicity and directness of a great writer, bringing back to us the very atmosphere of the pioneer days when men lived dangerously on the outskirts of civilization, the days of the covered wagon and the buffalo, back in the '70's.

JOHN LANE THE BODLEY HEAD LTD., VIGO STREET, W.1